MW00714227

Harry O. Long Jr.

Letters of

A TRUE STORY

Love

and

WAR

1944 - 1945

HARRY O. LANG, JR.

Sage
Creek
Press

Traverse City, Michigan

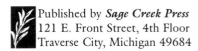Published by *Sage Creek Press*
121 E. Front Street, 4th Floor
Traverse City, Michigan 49684

Publisher's Cataloging-in-Publication Data
Lang, Harry O., Jr.
    Letters of love and war (1944-1945): a true story / Harry O.
Lang, Jr. -- Traverse City, MI : Sage Creek Press, 1998.
        p.   cm.
        ISBN 1-890394-26-2
    1. World War, 1939-1945—personal narratives, American.
    2. United States. Marine Corps—Biography.   3. World War,
    1939-1945—Pacific Area.   I. Title.
D811 .L36   1998   98-85197
940.54 ' 8373   dc—21   CIP

PROJECT COORDINATION BY JENKINS GROUP, INC.

02 01 00 99 ◆ 5 4 3 2 1

Printed in the United States of America

To Ginny
for the joy of the days and the blessings of children.
54 years after our first letter.

Contents

Contents

Prologue

$\mathcal{I}$n August of 1944, soon after he was graduated from Marine Corps Officers Training School, Harry O. Lang, Jr. headed home for a thirty-day leave. After his leave, he would travel to Camp Pendleton, California, before shipping out to the war in the Pacific theater. For Harry, "home" now meant Rochester, Michigan, where his parents had recently bought a gentleman's farm. His mother had been writing to him about the farm for several weeks -- and in her most recent letters, slipping in notes about their new neighbors, the McCulloughs, who had a 20-year-old daughter, Ginny. "She's such a sweet and charming young girl. And she'll still be on her summer break from Bennett Junior College, in Millbrook, New York, when you come home. Of course, you'll have to meet her, seeing as she's your new neighbor. Mrs. McCullough and I have it all arranged."

Warning bells clanged in Harry's head, but he shrugged them off and decided to indulge his mother. Still, he put off the meeting for over a week, and it wasn't until Mrs. McCullough herself called that he agreed to meet Ginny for a brief horseback ride, figuring he could claim his horsemanship woefully out of practice, if necessary, and be out in under an hour, no harm done. (For her part, Ginny, who shared the same wary view of anyone her mother would fix her up with, didn't even bother to dry her long, wavy brown hair and told her mother to "just let him in the back door.")

Within a few seconds of meeting her, however, Harry had already started plotting just how long he could stretch out that horseback ride. As he would admit eventually to his mother, "I was quite impressed." And he would later acknowledge to himself, "Ginny just fit into my life."

Ginny had felt the same spark, and the next few weeks flew by in a whirl of activity. Together, Harry and Ginny raced Ginny's horses across wide open fields. They plunged into the chilly water of a neighbor's pool for a frantic swim before dashing home to dry off in front of the fire. They watched movies, took in shows, went dancing -- and most of all laughed constantly, continually, uproariously.

One wet, gloomy Thursday, they were forced inside by the weather. Ginny dragged the phonograph down beside the huge fieldstone fireplace in her parents' living room. Her family was gone for the day; the house, for a change, was blissfully quiet. Outside, cold rain drizzled in a constant stream, and a biting wind gusted against the window panes. But Harry built a blazing fire, and Ginny cranked up Vaughn Monroe on the phonograph, and the combination drowned out the wind and distracted them from the cold. They spun through Ginny's entire collection of Monroe, then Glenn Miller, Tommy Dorsey and Frank Sinatra. They laughed easily, talked freely, and felt a perfect contentment, ignoring as best they could the thoughts that had simmered below the surface of their good times: the knowledge that with the world at war, this could be their last time together for months, for years -- or forever.

Harry wanted to tell Ginny how much these days had meant to him, how completely she had captivated him. Instead, he leaned over and gently kissed her.

The next day, Harry left for Camp Pendleton, reporting as a Second Lieutenant Rifle Platoon Leader in the Marine First Division. He was 22-years-old and on the first leg of a long journey to a lonely foxhole on the front lines of Okinawa, where in the bloodiest battle of the Pacific War, 38,000 Americans would be killed or wounded.

Before leaving, Harry promised Ginny he would write to her as often as he could. A similar promise was made to his mother and dad, who were anxious to hear also from Harry's brother Dick, serving in the Marine Corps as well. These are Harry's letters.

Acknowledgments

To Joseph Avenick for his devotion to have this story told.

To Doreen Naughton for her perceptive Prologue and Epilogue.

Part 1

Camp Pendleton, California
September 1944 — December 1944

Camp Pendleton is located on the coast between Los Angeles and San Diego. Its thousands of acres of terrain offer remote sites for simulated combat training. The training is intense, and the living conditions are rugged.

ॐ

September 23, 1944

𝒟ear Ginny,

Hope your letters will not be as late as my promise to write. I have been busy—without a place to write. I know you would understand if you were to mysteriously appear here all of a sudden and see the scattered tents flapping in the wind and dust, deep in the canyon: tents with dirt floors, canvas cots and candlelight. We have no hot water, and we eat mostly beans and stew. This is not a complaint. It's just that I wanted you to be able to picture me here—hoping you will think of it often. Three other fellows are also huddled around candles, writing letters to their girlfriends, wives, and relatives.

Ginny, I want you to know that you're guilty of making me take my mind off work—that you're guilty of making my recent leave the best I could ask for and much more than I ever expected. I was pretty poor at expressing and showing you how glad I felt about our time together; but in my mind, each thing that we did remains fresh with a yearning for it to happen all over again someday. Ginny, I'll never forget being in front of the fireplace on a cloudy afternoon—cozy, warm, and comfortable with you beside me. There will be horses to ride again, and swims we will take together again. I miss you. Write, Ginny, as often as you can. I'll do the same. Good night. Time to sleep.

But, before I doze off, it is time to remember how thankful and glad I am that we know each other, that we've spent time together, and that we'll spend time together again in the future.

৵

September 23, 1944

Dear Mother & Dad,

Just a note. Sorry to say just a note, but my candle is burning low. I'm now living in native conditions. Well, not quite. Our tents have dirt floors; and we are spread out over this desolate canyon, sort of part desert, and we sleep in canvas cots, cold water only, eating camp-type food out of mess kits. Doc, Jake, Bill Terry, and I share a tent. We've been assigned here with the infantry for 8 weeks of field training exercises.

I want to thank you for everything at home. Certainly enjoyed myself, together we had a swell time. If only Dick were there. Let's hope it won't be too long before the four of us are laughing together at the farm again.

Don't send my overcoat or anything, for I have every-

thing I need for now. Will write again soon. Good night....Love.

꙰

September 25, 1944

𝒟ear Ginny,

We saw California rain for the first time today, Ginny. No matter what part of the country it falls in, it's still depressing. Our uniforms are wet, and so are we. So much for the land of sunshine. Finally, at night, I'm dry for the first time today. Thinking of you keeps me from getting totally depressed. I'll write again soon.

꙰

September 27, 1944

𝒟*ear Mother & Dad,*

Here's your other Marine again. Didn't have a chance to mention much about my work. At present, I'm being instructed to teach my own troops about infantry tactics....
Getting away on liberty, finding enough food, and toilet facilities are all sore points. No liberty at night during weekdays, except for married men living off camp. We work until five each Saturday, so we arrive in Los Angeles about 9:30-10:00 dirty and hungry.
  Jake really has a set-up being married. He and Jeanne

have a nice place on the beach at Oceanside about 15 miles away. So each day at 5:00 P.M. he rides home with a fellow owning a car and returns the next morning for work. He gets a hot shower and decent food. We, however, have very little water (none hot), and we eat in a dusty tent where our food is scooped up and plopped in our mess kits. Oh well, there are hundreds of guys here under the same conditions... I've fond memories of home and how glad I'll be someday to be back at the farm.

Wrote Dick at his new Marine base. Looks like we'll be able to get together in Los Angeles. Have written Ginny. Think she's number one now....Love

౩

September 28, 1944

𝒟ear Ginny,

It's a beautiful night tonight, with fog setting as a blanket in the canyon. A bright, half-moon is reflecting from the fog. It's just cool enough for a wool shirt. There are coyotes gradually wandering nearer, yelling. I'm experiencing the smell of mellow tobacco coming from my pipe, and I have a candle for light. Some of the boys in the tent are undressing for bed; another is silently reading; one is packing laundry; and one more is puffing on his pipe. It's almost like home being with these fellows. Five of us have been bunking together for almost a year now, and I imagine we'll ship out together. I think of you often, Ginny. I wish we were back together in

Rochester. Our time was short, but it was long enough for me to realize my anxiety to be with you again, my yearning to hold you near.

꒰

October 1, 1944

𝒟ear Ginny,

In many ways, this place is like a prison. Day after day of the same routine—work, eat, sleep—work, eat, sleep—drains me more mentally than physically. The boys and I have to fig-ure out a way to get off of camp grounds on a regular basis. But, forget about my problems. Write me and tell me about yours. Use me as a sounding board. Maybe I can make you feel better.

꒰

Author's Note: Getting out of camp and into civilization wasn't easy. To ditch the dungarees and trench boots for a dress uniform and find the comfort of a hotel room and a decent meal motivated us to buy a car.

October 4, 1944

𝒟ear Ginny,

I couldn't be happier, because both of your letters came today. This camp isn't so bad after all! Life is suddenly brighter, and your letters are good for me. With a steady diet of your letters, I'd never have a bad day. That's how I feel, Ginny, as I sit on my canvas cot beside a flickering candle. I can picture you, priming yourself to study for your college courses, but my thoughts of home are more powerful. Christmas will be here before we know it. Too bad you can't have your horse with you. It must feel good to be a senior in college. Remember when you were a lowly freshman? So, you're into English. As I remember, some of those old English novels are rather spicy and humorous. Hope you don't have to suffer with the dry ones. A good novel needs a few sexy passages.

The boys in our tent all chipped in and bought a car yesterday in Los Angeles. It's a 1934 Pontiac, more an antique. But it runs, and we need one to use around here with everything so far apart and so far away.

Wouldn't it be great to be home together for Christmas? We'd have a dandy time living so close and hoping to be closer. I'll hop on that magic carpet and mentally be with you. I think I'll do that now as I crawl into bed.

ॐ

October 5, 1944

Dear Mother & Dad,
Well, we bought a car. A 1934 Pontiac for $175.00. Doc,
Bill Terry, Cal Tinsley (another tent-mate), and I split the
cost. But getting gas is a problem. We can get only an "A"
book of coupons. With L.A. 75 miles away, that's not

enough. But don't worry, folks, we'll get gas somehow….
Looks like Dick will meet us in L.A. so we can celebrate his
birthday.

As for my work, I'm doing fine. Despite my gripes about
conditions, I've been very conscientious about my work of
being an instructor. Public speaking never caused me much
trouble, and I've taken pride in trying to give a better, more
interesting lecture than the next fellow. When I get my own
platoon, I'm really going to be prepared for them as far as
understanding infantry work.

Have received two very encouraging letters from Ginny.
She writes very intelligently, with a hint of romance. I'm
actually sincerely interested in her. After the war, I'll really
be ready to spend lots of time, getting to know her better….

So, folks, the candle is burning to only a flicker, cold is
passing through the canyon, coyotes have begun their yelp-
ing and not more than five minutes ago a cute baby skunk
was rubbing, as a cat, against my leg while I'm writing you.
Doc jumped so much he scared it out. My canvas cot looks
nice and warm. Good night….Love.

ᘓ

October 9, 1944

Dear Ginny,

Driving the Pontiac is an adventure. We're never sure if it
will start. We have to pray it will get us back to camp on
time. But it gets us where we want to go—to L.A. I'd like to

show you this town, Ginny. But first I have to come back alive. Good night for now, darling.

♍

October 12, 1944

𝒟ear Ginny,

Your Marine is decrepit right now. I'm laid up with a spot of tonsillitis. A few days of rest supplemented by the usual sulfur pills ought to do the trick. I don't mind the rest. But my throat feels like it has a red-hot watermelon in it.

Your Marine bought another car. This time it's a 1936 Ford. The Pontiac died on us. We all chipped in again. It looks pretty good from the outside, although the inside is pretty shabby. Driving it back to camp, there were moments when it would stall out. It chugged along, though—much better than the Pontiac. We only need a car until we ship out, of course.

I had intended to meet my brother this weekend—after changing plans no less than what seemed like a thousand times. I received a letter from him today saying that he had been caught gambling after taps and was put on two weeks' restriction. If I send a telegram saying it is imperative that I see him, then he says the chaplain may intercede and make him free for the weekend. At any rate, he won 120 dollars, the lucky stiff.

I've often tried to picture your school with those brown, yellow, and red-covered hills of the fall season—with the smell of football in the air. If I were back at Colgate, we'd have a great time together: with football games, house parties, maybe a trip to New York City—and, before long, some skiing. But enough of this fantasy! It's time to go to bed. Keep writing. You'll never know how good it feels to come back from the field tired and dirty to find your letter waiting. It's better than a warm shower.

რ

October 15, 1944

*D*ear Ginny,

I know your letters are due soon. Thinking that your words, on paper, will be waiting for me at the end of the work day is the only thing that can keep me going with a smile on my face. If you ever stopped writing to me, I don't know what I'd do. Your letters are my life now, period.

რ

October 17, 1944

*D*ear Ginny,

It was a luxury receiving your letter on Saturday and yet another letter today. And I really appreciate it, knowing you're so busy at school. Be sure to send me your brother's address as soon as you're able, and I'll do my best to find him. I'm keeping my eyes open for him around here.

Your New York City trip sounded dandy, Ginny. It is quite a thrill for me whenever I go there. Hope you noticed that Colgate beat Cornell last Saturday.

While lying in the sun for a few minutes this afternoon, I shut my eyes and transported myself back to remembering swimming together, then on the horses for a ride, and finally it was Thursday next to the fireplace. I'd give anything for that to happen all over again. Maybe it will, before too many years.

Pretty tired tonight, so I'll say good night for now.

ॐ

October 19, 1994

Dear Ginny,

I had a dream last night, Ginny. I dreamt we were skiing together. It was probably a reaction to the heat wave here in camp. I guess California weather is preparing us for the steamy South Pacific, where we'll be headed before too long. I miss you, Ginny, with or without the snow skis.

ॐ

Author's Note: There is a special sense of bonding among those of us who have been living and training together for these many months.

Camp Pendleton, California

October 21, 1944

*D*ear Ginny,

It's another sunshine-filled day in California—and another day when I wish I could be alongside you watching a football game and wearing sporty fall clothes. I'm not complaining, for I guess I could be in worse places. I'm only sort of dreaming.

I'm losing two of my best friends. These are fellows I've been with since I joined the service. A runner came out in the field the other day asking for volunteers for troop transport quartermaster. These fellows raised their hands, and so they are moving to another camp tomorrow—making it the first time we've been separated. Naturally, there has been a lot of kidding between us about it. I say they are not tough enough for the infantry, and they retaliate saying they'll visit me after the war in my six-by-three-foot box six-feet under. Despite the kidding, we feel a little sentimental about their leaving. Doc was Jake's best man, and I was an usher at his wedding in Washington. Even though Jake was married, the three of us spent almost every weekend together somewhere. Troop transport quartermaster entails a lot of ship-loading work. And as for myself, this would drive me crazy. It's strictly a non-combat outfit, but you'd probably see the end of the war by being in it. But something inside me said, "Don't raise your hand, Harry." Infantry is rough and dirty, but there is a deep personal satisfaction with having your platoon of men and being able to train them as you see fit. Also, it's a challenge to see what you can do with them in combat. If I can successfully take my platoon through several combat operations and return to the States safe and sound (with very few casualties among my men), I'd really feel as if I had accomplished something meaningful. It would be the greatest experience I could hope for. I'm not trying to hail myself as a hero. It's just the way I feel. Confidence is half the battle.

Received my presidential ballot from the Avon County city clerk today, which means I'll vote for another straight Republican ticket. I'm Tom Dewey's strongest supporter around here. Of course, dad feels the same way. I have a hunch you feel the same way. It's time for some new blood in the White House. But I guess I've rambled long enough. I'm hoping for the time when we'll be home together again.

჻

October 22, 1944

Dear Mother & Dad,
Was real good to talk to you yesterday morning. As you said, it seems that I've been away for months, when it's been just over four weeks.

Most disappointing was Dick not being able to get away, especially when I had a dandy program all set up, and it was Dick's twenty-first birthday. I couldn't help swearing at the Marine Corps. We went ahead with our plans any-way....

I've had two opportunities to transfer from infantry to

troop transport quartermaster (loading ships — logistics), which is pretty clean living and non-combat duty. It was tempting, believe me, while living here during the week dirty and hungry, but I'm too proud to be an officer in the infantry to consider it. Jake and Doc volunteered for it. With Jake being married and Doc being his friend since college days, I guess I can understand. Trouble is, it breaks us up after being together for so long. Bill Terry stuck by me, so at least we'll be together....

Mother, some of your cookies would hit the spot.... The more Ginny writes, the more I like her....Love.

༄

October 24, 1944

𝒟ear Ginny,

First cool night in quite a while. It's peaceful. Maybe a calm before the storm. I'm getting more confidence in what I'm learning to do, and this ability to perform is giving me more confidence in other areas. I'm even standing taller now. And when I talk to people, I'm straightforward, to the point, no nonsense. There's definitely something to say about Marine training. It works. I know that personally now.

༄

October 27, 1944

$\mathcal{D}$ear Ginny,

A bright moon tonight. It's shining over you, also. Only for you, it shines through crisp, cool autumn air. You're in bed now, Ginny, all cozy and warm, sound asleep. A pretty picture, a pretty girl. A thought to you from this guy wishing we were close, so close that a kiss would be inevitable.

ꕔ

November 1, 1944

$\mathcal{D}$ear Ginny,

It's a cloudy day—unusual for California. I enjoyed it, because it's more like Michigan or New York. Sorry I didn't write last Friday as I said I would. But we had a night field problem that lasted almost until daybreak. It's a luxury coming out of the field and finding your letters waiting for me. I know you're busy what with studying for courses and with activities, and I appreciate the time you find to write.

Just a few minutes ago we were called to a meeting for more volunteers for transport quartermaster. Even though I possess a good duty report, once again I would not raise my hand. That something in the back of my head is still saying "DON'T DO IT, HARRY!"

We have our car running O.K. now. Except we ran out of gas coupons. In Los Angeles we had a flat, ran out of oil, and ran out of gas all within an hour. But the car runs, and it got us back to camp on time (fifteen minutes before morning roll call). I really enjoyed seeing my brother, Dick. He looks fine, and we raised a little harmless hell together. We went to Ciro's, and then on Sunday we found the Palladium. Xavier Cugat was at Ciro's, and Woody Herman at the Palladium. Jake and Jeanne and Doc were with us. It was a great time. I kept looking at the empty seat next to me at Ciro's, hoping I could somehow transport you there so you could be sitting next to me.

৵

November 3, 1944

*D*ear Ginny,

I was in a lazy mood today. This afternoon I took my class of about nine sergeants out in the field to rehearse a demon-stration for Monday. We worked until about five minutes before three o'clock. Then I told them to take a fifteen-minute break. I put my head down, too, and I thought I'd shut my eyes for just a minute or two. The next thing I knew, one of the sergeants was tapping me on the bottom of my foot. I opened my eyes and looked up, half awake. Then the sergeant said, "Sir, it's ten minutes after four." I had slept an hour and fifteen minutes while they sat around waiting for me to wake up. A fine example I am.

I'm not going to Los Angeles this weekend, even though we get off Friday night until Monday. That Hollywood bal-lyhoo was exciting at first, but there is something about it that's uncomfortable. I think it's because everything appears so artificial and unreal. It's hard to picture anyone leading a normal everyday life there in Hollywood. Most of the time it reminds me of a three-ring circus. Instead of Hollywood, I'll be spending the weekend with Jake and Jeanne, at their invitation. We'll play some golf and swim a little. But, whatever I'll be doing, for each moment I'll be wishing that you were there with me.

ॐ

November 4, 1944

Dear Mother & Dad,
Well at last Dick and I made connections. He really looked good (the same ole Dick). Jake and Doc (they won't be trans-ferred for awhile) and Bill Terry joined us — as did Jake's wife, Jeanne. We really tried to show Dick a good time. Sorry we were unable to call you Sunday. The operator said there would be a 5-7 hour delay. As far as I can see, Dick has a good duty and ought to remain safe throughout the war. Saw his Sigma Nu ring, and it's a dandy.

This weekend we get Friday night to Monday morning off. I'm kind of fed up with the Hollywood ballyhoo of Los Angeles, so I'm planning on going to Laguna Beach. It's about 20 miles away, being one of the prettiest towns on the coast. Thought I'd do some shopping, swim, and rest.

Monday I pick up a company of recruits to spend a week instructing them in infantry tactics. Evidently, I'm going to be an instructor for the next month or so.

Dad, you'd better get hot with that shotgun of yours. You own a hundred acres of land, wait all year for hunting season, and then can't hit a damn thing. We'll have a little training session when I get home.... I've been bribing the gas station guy with cigarettes.... Still hear from Ginny (every day, in fact)....Love.

༃

November 5, 1944

𝒟ear Ginny,

Can't get you out of my mind. But it's not like thoughts of you are a distraction. To the contrary. I feel stronger when I remember the good times we had together. You pray for me, and I'll pray that the good times return.

༃

Author's Note: Marines must be tough enough to fight but smart enough to win.

November 7, 1944

𝒟ear Ginny,

Finally, I have my platoon of men. Each morning I meet them at the crossroads, where we march out to the field. From seven o'clock in the morning until six at night I instruct them in every phase of infantry tactics. For lunch, we eat K rations. At night, the supper is cold. They're a fine bunch of kids—all about 18 or 19 years old. They all seem genuinely interested in learning how to be infantrymen. But every once in awhile I've got to yell at them—reminding them of the importance of their work. Each hour they get a ten-minute rest period. When the end of the day finally arrives, we're not too proud to admit we're tired and ready for bed. When I finally do crawl into my bunk, I sleep with a satisfaction that at last I'm really doing something worthwhile. Instructing them, I'm sure, will give them all a better chance to come out of this war safe and sound. I'm going to stay awake tonight as long as I can with the thoughts of the poem you wrote for me. In fact, I'm going to write one and send it back to you. Here it is:

There are times when I feel I'll never see
A face so lovely as yours to me
With hopes and dreams I've lived each day
At night for those things I softly pray

What they are and where they'll be
Plays on my mind like a symphony
A little white house with shutters green
Ivy scattered and trees so lean

Sunshine shines and sometime rain
Peace and quiet shall always remain
Gracefully she wanders there alone
Waiting patiently for him to come home

There are things to talk about and lots to do
A love that continues to be ever new
Children will come and plans to be made
Sailboats to be sailed and golf will be played

Camp Pendleton, California

Horses to ride and nights to have fun
A pipe to smoke when the day is done
Those are the things that to me are great
I'm sorry they will have to come a little late

So I'll fight hard for all those things
Content to know the happiness it brings
If something should happen I want this to show
That I'll never be the guy you used to know.

This poem adequately expresses my thoughts, I think. Meanwhile, I'm reminded that it may be a long time before we're together again. Also, it will only be a few days before the censors start reading our letters. It'll feel kind of funny knowing that someone else is reading my thoughts about you. Keep that in mind when you read the letters that follow. I hope you're saving them all. If any of my words have been cut out, I'll try to remember what I said.

ॐ

November 10, 1944

Dear Ginny,

Despite all the training I'm getting, I can't help but wonder what exactly will be different when I finally get into combat. The officers who are training us don't talk much about their experiences. I have a hunch some of them might not have had any (or very little) combat time. I sure hope they know what they're talking about. I also hope that all the good officers didn't die in the South Pacific.

࿐

November 16, 1944

𝒟ear Ginny,

I'm in a replacement draft, which, to you I know, means very little. I'm in a group of about four-hundred men, and we are being equipped for overseas combat duty. Our draft is to leave the country December 1st and go directly to what is called a staging area. There I will train while awaiting a call. When a Second Lieutenant rifle platoon leader is killed or becomes seriously wounded in a current combat area, I will be called to take his place. That is, to take over his platoon and continue on with the infantry operation. Military organizations at the present are such that they are no longer forming new units as a regiment or division. Consequently, they are retaining old organizations by replacing their casualties by members of a replacement draft.

I've no right to believe I won't be killed, because each second, minute, hour, and day men are dying. And I could someday be one of them. But I'll remain the optimist I've always been, hoping for the best and feeling that it will eventually come. I'm not going to try and be a hero—only do my best and do it well.

So, Ginny, I will be going farther away from you for awhile to the South Pacific. With censorship, I will be able to say little of a military matter in my letters. That little poem explains what I want most of all, and I'll be dreaming of that picture in the poem and remembering you and how without you that picture would never be complete. Because, I love you. You're the essence of everything I want.

I'll come back to you, my family, and the farm—kissing you, holding you, and never wanting to let you go. I promise.

My platoon is just about ready to ship out, but there are two more companies to be formed yet.

Our mail is lost. I'm lonely from the absence of your letters. It's been two weeks now. Midnight is drawing close, and time is getting shorter. I want to hear your words. I want to be near you. But the time without you is going to be so very long.

ぅ

November 16, 1944

Dear Mother & Dad,

My platoon is off on a work detail this morning, so it leaves me some time to write and explain what's happening now as far as a replacement draft is concerned.

I have a platoon of men that I am equipping for overseas, making certain they have all the proper gear. When the replacement draft, constituting about 1,300 men, is ready we will board ship and sail for what is called a staging area. It will be in the South Pacific somewhere. I will train my men, acclimatizing them to the area. Then, we will be called to whatever is needed as a replacement.

So, I will be leaving the country for awhile, folks, but please don't worry about me. I've been training for over 18

months how to take care of myself, and I've got all the confidence necessary to do it. There will be a time now when my
letters will be far apart and they will be censored.

As mentioned before, Bill Terry and I are rooming together and we still have our car, which we will soon have to get
rid of. I finally wiggled a "B" book of gas coupons out of the
ration board, so we will have enough gas to last us. Jake and
Doc are here this morning. We've said goodbye. They're shipping out to San Francisco tomorrow morning. Jake said
goodbye to Jeanne last night. Parting with good friends is
tough.

Wrote Ginny about what's happening....Love.

꒝

November 22, 1944

Dear Ginny,

There's a certain excitement now, with all of the guys,
including me, a little edgy. It's not so much a nervous energy
or one based on fear. We feel quietly optimistic. We know
we'll give it our best shot in the South Pacific, wherever
we're headed. And if God is with us, we'll find our way
home again.

꒝

November 22, 1944

Dear Mother & Dad,

Just a note before going to bed on the eve of Thanksgiving to say I wish I could wake up tomorrow morning and find myself at the farm with the four of us all together. Knowing this is only a flighty dream, I hope next year at this time it will be true.

Wrote Dick again in hopes that we can get together for a weekend....

Please don't feel disturbed about my future, folks. When you look back, I've been in the States three years since war was declared, and we must consider that as being pretty lucky.

Thanks a lot for the fudge. Bill Terry says thanks also....Love.

ى

November 26, 1944

Dear Ginny,

In talking with the guys in my platoon, I find that they have a lot in common with each other, and with me, as far as morals are concerned. They all believe in some kind of almighty power, regardless of their religions. And they're all praying.

ى

November 30, 1944

𝒟ear Ginny,

My platoon is finally all ready now, and from today on I should have plenty of spare time until we embark. I heard some news that our ship is not due in the harbor until December 12th. But I don't know how true it is. I'm going to see my brother, Dick, this weekend. We finally arranged our liberties to coincide.

Finally, I wiggled some more gas coupons out of the ration board. I found a gas certificate from the first car we had that I forgot to give back to the used car dealer. So we gave it to one of the guys. He told the ration board that he was married, and his wife lived at the address of the previous owner, whose name was on the certificate. And that she (her name was Blossom Achein, entirely unknown to us) said that he could use the coupons to drive back and forth to Los Angeles in order to see his wife. After filling out the necessary forms (forging some names) we got the board to examine the application. They sent it off to Oceanside to be verified, then we received the good result of eight B coupons. We've become con artists. Legally, we've run the car on six A coupons. We've bought black market gas, appealed a lot to the sympathy of gas station attendants, begged, borrowed, about everything for some coupons. It's been fun and worthwhile. But I don't think we'll take any more chances. It's just too risky.

I've thought of home, of you, and I've heard White Christmas played so many times on the radio. I'm in an impatient sort of a way tonight. Despite the thought of an uncertain future, I'm anxious to go overseas and get it over with instead of waiting around knowing it's impossible to return home again until the war is history.

There is something I should say to you, Ginny. Possibly our short acquaintance doesn't warrant such a reaction as that has occurred. So I want you to know that I have meant everything that I've said to you. I haven't built you up to be merely a dream or a person I've picked to satisfy a love impulse just because I felt I needed someone to pour my heart out to. It's not the product of war time conditions. You've made me this way, because I can't stop thinking about you. At night in bed I wish you were near to hold tenderly. When it rains, I yearn for you to be next to me beside a fireplace. On clear, fresh, sunny days, I want you outside with me, enjoying it—every place, all the time, everywhere.

I am going to see my brother tomorrow. Also, the fellow I room with, Bill Terry, is meeting his brother. So, all of us ought to have a good time.

I'm pretty tired tonight. I gave my platoon some physical exercise today and damn near killed myself. Guess I needed it worse than they did. Hopefully, I'll be in top shape before I ship out.

I re-read your latest letter and also the old ones. I am willing to do anything and everything to get this war over with. Without your letters, I don't know what I'd do. Good luck with the horse show, Ginny. Hope you capture all the honors. I'll bet you will. Thinking of you as always.

❧

December 4, 1944

𝒟ear Ginny,

Still no definite word on when we're shipping out. The rumors are flying, though. All of my instincts tell me we'll be out of California before Christmas. As this unknown date draws nearer, I want to be with you even more. Hope those thoughts don't make me a coward.

❧

December 7, 1944

𝒟ear Ginny,

Notice the date, Ginny. Three years ago today in 1941, the Japs bombed Pearl Harbor, and look where we are today, sending thousands of troops against them, backed right up to their homeland where they belong.

Maybe we will stop at Pearl on the way over. I understand you can still see much of the damage. Seeing what was done as a cowardly act will give us even greater inspiration.

I'll never forget that day for another reason. It was on December 7, 1941 that I was initiated into my fraternity at Colgate. That date is engraved on the back of my pin, which I've left with mother and dad.

We will have other memories from what lies ahead. The ones I'm looking forward to are the ones to be spent with you.

༝

December 10, 1944

Dear Mother & Dad,
It was wonderful talking to you. I'm sorry if it must be the last time for awhile. Talked to Ginny, too, at her school in Millbrook, N. Y.

As mentioned, I've been awfully busy this week with my platoon. It's at full strength now — 63 men (1 staff sergeant, 4 corporals, 32 privates first class, and the rest privates.) It's like taking care of an overgrown family....

No matter where I'll be, I'll still have my Christmas. Your presents are all packed in my bag. Am sending one of my bags home. Don't open it until Christmas. Will write soon....Love.

༝

December 11, 1944

Dear Ginny,
Bill Terry, my roommate, took the car up to Los Angeles to sell. I almost cried, saying good-bye to it after becoming so attached. We called it "Baby," because we had to pet it and use kind words to keep it going. I really learned quite a bit about mechanics from it. Bill and I were the only ones that could drive it, since we knew its bad habits and what was necessary to correct them. I'm all tired out from walking for a change (not really). The tires had large patches of wear, but we had only one flat tire, and that was because we drove

over one of those small safety zones we were unable to see. The upholstering was as poor as could be, all ripped, torn, and worn. The back seat floor was constantly filled with oil cans, morning papers, tools, rags, magazines, etc. And it smoked like a train engine, thick and black. It was a real character that everyone in camp knew on sight. It always got us where we wanted to go.

I'm kind of homesick tonight after writing the folks and my brother. Guess I'm not much of a hard-boiled, leatherneck Marine really. My family is too good not to shed a tear about. I worry how they'll feel and what they'll do if I never come back. And, darling, thinking of you and glancing at your picture makes me so warm and comfortable and happy and glad.

ى

Author's Note: How can I stop thinking that there may be no returning?

December 13, 1944

Dear Ginny,

Am leaving tomorrow morning early. My deepest, most sincere thoughts will be of you always. I'll treasure our memories and dreams of the future. You will be with me in everything I do. I know you are fine, wonderful, and real. You are kind, honest, true, warm, and tender. I want to hold you tight, kiss you, and say "Good-bye for now, darling. I'll be back soon. Merry Christmas and Happy New Year."

Part 2

Aboard Troop Transport Ship
December 1944 — January 1945

December 22, 1944

*D*ear Ginny,

I've been on the transport ship for over a week now. Life aboard so far has been very comfortable despite some trouble with my stomach the first couple of days. I thought I'd never stop rocking back and forth and bouncing up and down. I must confess I came aboard with a belly full of bourbon and soda after a last night party with the boys we were leaving behind. Certainly, I'll know better next time. Fortunately, my friend, Bill Terry, and I are in the same stateroom— ample with space, comfortable bunks, and toilet. Duties aboard are few, consisting mainly of a two-hour watch every twenty-four hours. So, I've found plenty of time to read and rest and bask in the tropical sun and the balmy breezes of the South Pacific—watching flying fish, an occasional shark, or a passing ship.

You will note on the envelope that my letters are now censored. Just wrote mother and dad mentioning I'd hoped you had been over to see them. Often during the day I picture your home and mine covered with snow—and both filled with Christmas cheer.

I have such a strong yearning to be there, that I have to think of something else suddenly—or I have to force myself to start reading. I miss your letters so much, darling. Your picture is with me all the time between two pieces of cardboard in my wallet. Certainly, I wish your large picture would arrive. I hope my package to you arrived in time for Christmas. Good night for now. I'll write again as soon as we find another port. While you are home, pretend it was last

September and on a Thursday sitting before the fireplace playing records. Remember?

࿓

December 22, 1944

Dear Mother & Dad,
Now it's life abroad a transport, bound for an unknown destination....

It's hard to realize it's Christmas time when I can feel a tropical sun and balmy breezes. But, many times a day I picture the farm covered now with snow, the Christmas tree all bright with good cheer surrounded with presents wrapped with care. I have your presents ready to open and hope you received and enjoy my presents....

Hope Ginny came over to see you while she was home from school. I've become quite fond of her and real anxious to know her better. Her letters are great and what she says even better....Love.

࿓

December 24, 1944

Dear Ginny,
It's Christmas Eve aboard a transport ship, and it feels a little spooky. A few of us sang carols out on the deck. But no

matter how hard we sang, we couldn't bring on any snow or Santa and his reindeer. This is the warmest Christmas Eve I've ever experienced. The temperature feels like it should be May or June. I'm praying that I'll see a cold Christmas Eve again one of these years—with you right next to me. Your smile will be the only warmth I'll need.

᧭

December 29, 1944

Dear Mother and Dad,
Still sailing the ocean blue. Just returned from up on the deck where Bill Terry and I felt the cool breezes of a bright full moon glistening on almost motionless water. It would have been quite romantic if Ginny were with me.

Christmas, naturally, was an unusual one. Thanks so very much for your presents. I have that little Christmas tree perched on top of my bed lamp, with the dictionary beside me now (something I really needed). The fruit cake and candy sure hit the spot and, of course, I enjoyed the books, along with the picture of the farm as it appeared on Christmas day. So, folks, you really gave me a Merry Christmas as always. Sure do appreciate it....

Hope you saw Ginny. Be sure not to worry....Love.

᧭

January 4, 1945

$\mathcal{D}$ear Ginny,

Just returned from the quarterdeck portside where the moon appears to be almost half now, glistening in small patches on the Pacific. The ocean is quiet tonight, barely moving from a soft, warm, tropical breeze. After supper, Bill Terry and I always go out on the deck for some fresh air. Every night brings up a different topic of conversation. Usually, though, it always hinges around past experiences and our post-war dreams of the future. All the things we've thought about during the day are confessed at this time each night. Some are silly, other quite possible. It is always the most enjoyable part of the day. Most of the time we return to our stateroom, undress, climb into our bunks, turn on the reading lamp and read.

There is a fellow aboard, Norm White, who grew up with me in Detroit. He's one of our old gang who helped build our cabin. He was deferred for engineering until he was graduated from college. Then he joined the Marines. While I'm on watch every day, he visits me. We spend these two-hour shifts reminiscing high school days and the fun we've had staying at the cabin.

I saw a shark the other day, and I'm constantly watching for flying fish. Outside of that, blue water is the only scenery available.

I hope you received the letters I sent while we were in a port. I had a sailor mail them for me. He was able to get off the ship. I also hope that you enjoyed Christmas and that my presents arrived on time. Our Christmas was as you can imagine, darling, a little unusual—although I did manage a Christmas drink or two. (Bill and I smuggled a few drinks aboard.) On Christmas Day I opened up a few presents I'd saved that the folks had sent. We sang carols again, read, and played cards. I've read *Rebecca* by Daphne Du Maurier. Also such books as *Good-bye Mr. Chips*; *Winesburg, Ohio* by Sherwood Anderson; and *The Theatre* by Somerset Maugham. All were good, but my favorite is *A Tree Grows In Brooklyn*. The rather sexy scenes in the books sure don't help my frustrations, which seem to grow by the day.

It's going to be quite some time before I can be with you again. Each minute at present brings me farther away, but only in distance. And the sooner I get there, the sooner I'll return. So, I'm going farther only to return sooner. Today is your birthday, darling, and I wish you the best always.

⌒

January 7, 1944

Dear Ginny,

The scuttlebutt throughout the ship is that we'll arrive tomorrow at an island where we'll do a last bit of training before going into combat. Funny thing about tropical islands. I've always thought I might like to sit under palm trees and have coconuts fall into my lap. Never thought I'd be working on a tropical island and fighting to stay alive.

Part 3

Pavuvu, South Pacific
January 1945 — March 1945

Author's Note: I doubt if the average person has heard of Pavuvu. It is in the Russell Islands and not far from the Solomon Islands, known for the battle of Guadalcanal. Pavuvu served as a hideaway base for the next invasion.

ᔓ

January 9, 1945

Dear Ginny,

Rain softly falls on the tent roof—and coconut trees sway from a tropical breeze that comforts these tired limbs (that are also sunburned). Right now I can hear music coming from the officers' club radio.

I picked up my platoon and boarded ship for another island—where we went through infantry operations. Now we've returned to this camp, where most of the comforts of home are close at hand.

Tonight we were asked how we wished our steaks cooked. The meal ended with ice cream and cake. I was certainly surprised to find conditions so civil. I can't complain about a thing, and I consider it a fortunate assignment. The work I'm doing is what I've always hoped for. I'm what is called a rifle platoon leader. The men are equipped with every kind of small arms weapon. It's exciting to be directing all this firepower, to be the leader. I'm mother, father, and teacher to my men. It's a great responsibility. The satisfaction derived from helping them become better infantry men is a great reward.

I'm in the First Division, which gained its fame on Guadalcanal and Cape Gloucester. They returned not long ago from Peleliu, where they suffered highly. I'm mighty proud to be part of this division.

Bill Terry and I are separated now for the first time in a year-and-a-half. He was assigned to a reconnaissance platoon that goes on an island several days before an invasion to sneak around and gain information on the enemy. This is important to us before we attack. Quite exciting work, I'd say. But Scotty and I are still together and live in the same tent. He has a rifle platoon also. So we manage to meet and have our fun at the club tent after work and talk about the States.

Tonight has been my first opportunity to relax and let my thoughts wander back to you. Walking down to the docks this morning, fresh and clear, I thought of you all the way. I was wondering what you were doing at that particular moment, what you were wearing, saying, and if you were thinking of a certain Marine and how much he was wishing he were near you. Every morning I will be walking down that road to board a landing craft for another island until we go off for our important operation, which is not far away. So maybe, Ginny, you can stop along your way and picture this guy in dungarees, pack, and rifle walking along thinking of you. I would like to tell you more about our island and my platoon. And I could, since I'm in charge of censoring all the mail. But there is the possibility of the enemy intercepting our mail. Then, they would gain valuable information that could cost lives.

You and thoughts of you mean everything to me, darling. And without you, I'd feel empty inside. It's time to go to bed now. Taps is sounding. No matter what happens out here, remember I love you and everything wonderful and pure and beautiful you stand for. Thursday afternoons and each other moment we were together still linger as my favorite memories and always shall.

ᴣ

January 10, 1945

Dear Mother & Dad,

Here I sit ten thousand miles from home. And with thoughts of you both and the farm. Coconut trees and bushy headed natives abound, though with military presence, it's not what you'd call a tropical paradise. However, our tents have electric lights. The superb food, along with a thick mattress, leaves no complaints. When in the field on maneuvers, it's C rations for chow, and we sleep in a hammock tied between coconut trees.

As I imagined and hoped for, I'm now officially a rifle platoon leader. After almost two years of training, I've the most honorable job in the military. And, I'm mighty proud of it. I've a good platoon, anxious to learn. Some of them are even combat veterans....

Now, be sure not to worry about me. I'm so well protected by a well-trained division and an enormous navy that it is needless to worry a bit.

Our mail is way behind. Wish I could read a letter from you and Ginny....

Tomorrow we're going to another island to practice with tanks. We leave at daybreak, so I'd better go to bed. Good night....Love.

ॐ

January 13, 1945

Dear Ginny,

As I've mentioned before, I'm awfully interested and quite excited about my work. If the war ends with myself able to go home again, this will be one of the greatest experiences a man could have. It will be great not in the sense that it shall be a cherished memory, but great from a humanistic standpoint. Men are men out here—so thoroughly interested in fighting for what they believe is right that you can't help admiring everyone of them for their spirit. Now that I'm here, I'm kind of anxious to see combat. Be sure to follow the news and the newsreels about the First Marine Division—for I will be there, and when we strike I'm sure you'll be surprised and happy. It should be the beginning of the end for Japan (bless their dirty hides).

I hope school is coming along all right. I imagine it's pretty difficult to get back to work after vacation. Soon it will be Easter and then summertime again. You'll be a graduate. Have you been riding lately? Perhaps there is too much snow. I'll bet it seemed good for you to see your horse again.

Please don't worry about me, darling. If anything should happen and I die, you'll know it was for you and the family. But let's not look at it that way. Let's keep hoping for the time when we can spend Thursdays by the fire again, when we can ride into the fields, when we can be together again. I know it's hard for you to keep writing, Ginny. Perhaps not so now. But when weeks turn to months, and months turn to a year or two, you may find there isn't much to say to me anymore except for the daily news or the weather. When the thrill of our short acquaintance begins to fade, you may yearn for other associations. Back home where conditions are civilized, human nature still controls. And things like that are apt to happen all very normally.

So, darling, if you find that so after a while, don't worry about it. Out here it's different. Memories of you and happy expectations of a future together all remain strong during the day. At night, I use every moment I can spare to remember. It's late now, so I'll close, darling. Hope your letters start coming. I love you.

ॐ

January 16, 1945

𝒟ear Ginny,

Training, training, training. I didn't think I'd be training here as long as I have. Looks like combat is not as close at hand as I thought it would be. All the delay does, though, is increase the tension. When my men get that weird look in their eyes, I just work them a little harder. Physical exertion seems to kill some of the tension.

〜

Author's Note: Loneliness plays tricks.

January 17, 1945

𝒟ear Ginny,

Received two more letters from you today. Although the letter I wrote last night still remains here on my desk waiting to be picked up, I had to say a few words to you tonight.

Went to a movie and saw *Government Girl*. I'd seen it before, but I felt I needed to see it again so I could relax tonight after chasing tanks all day through mud and rain. Usually it takes most of the evening for me to censor all the mail. Tonight, though, I called a night off, intending to go to bed early. I am lonely. I try to be stoic about it. Tonight, though, darling, I am lonely, and I want you to know you're guilty. Men sometimes after being overseas let their imaginations run away with them. They compensate for their loneliness that way. I can see it clearly in the letters I censor each night. Especially with men who have been here for two years or so. Sometimes they imagine their wife's unfaithfulness. Others write to girls they have never seen after getting addresses from friends. All of a sudden, she becomes the girl of his dreams, and he is content to think so. There are numerous examples, Ginny, all rather harmless, but some-

times with the drastic result of disillusionment. Being disil-
lusioned even brings satisfaction to these men at times. It
reminds them that they are human with emotional capabili-
ties. Instead of being routine machines driven each day,
working by habit, they can suffer, and suffering shows
them that they still have feelings.

I don't know exactly why I speak of such things. Perhaps
it's because I've recognized it. I don't want to become a life-
less machine nor a victim of flighty imagination. And
tonight I know that this loneliness is something deep and
very true; that the reason for the loneliness is because of
you.

Glad you had a chance to be with some of your friends
while you were home. And especially that my letter from
Pearl Harbor arrived so soon. It took exactly three days. Of
course, we're a long way from Pearl Harbor now. Mother
mentioned that you called a couple of times. I'm glad you
had a chance to talk to her, Ginny. She really appreciates
things like that more than ever with both Dick and I gone.
Hope your picture arrives soon.

I'll say good night now, Ginny, feeling much better now
that I've talked with you.

જ

January 19, 1945

Dear Ginny,
I know this letter will never be able to explain or express the

feelings inside of me—the happiness that overcame me when your four letters finally arrived today. I felt every word of them, darling, every little thing you said, the love and sincerity and pureness, so unaffected, so real and worthwhile. Don't ever change your style, Ginny. Every part of you is more than a man could ask for. You'll never realize how very happy you've made me. Now I am able to go on with even greater spirit. And the yearning I have for you was even more clearly realized from the loneliness for you and the effect of your letters. It's you that's going to keep me going out here. And yes, you did make me homesick when you spoke of a snowcovered countryside and the fireplace. But it felt good to be reminded of such things. The good life is there for me to return to.

Our main camp is in the center of a coconut plantation that was once owned by an Australian soap company. Remains of the main house and the equipment they used to process coconut oil are still to be seen. Their employees were the natives of this island and a neighboring island. Some of the natives are still here and are building a strawthatched chapel not too far from my tent. They also help on the docks unloading supplies. They smile all the time and they still retain some strange manners. The men hug each other and bump bellies. They wear burlap shirts and walk in bare feet. They've seen us soldiers saluting, and now they salute each other. It's laughable, really. Most of their natural habitat I see each day as we ride to other islands for field work. I see them in their villages, and I watch them in the water spearing fish. All the natives have skin as black as coal, with bushy hair. A few days ago I saw a group of them circle a rat and gradually move in to capture it. After which they immediately skinned it, each then taking a bloody bite as it was passed around. Also, they eat their fish raw upon spearing them. I suppose good American food like meat loaf would probably give them indigestion. The coconut trees are still very fruitful, and often my runner will split open a coconut to share with me. The ones in the shade are best, because the milk is cool. Birds of all colors and noises constantly follow the troops and appear as tropical as seen in the zoo. Of course, there are numerous ants, some good old American house flies, and the most obnoxious of all—the land crabs who come each night in armies of hundreds. Even our bunks are not safe, as they crawl everywhere. Three nights ago one the size of an apple crawled under the covers with me and stayed the entire night. I didn't discover him until I was making the bed in the morning.

It's getting late, and the unwritten law about putting our lights out here in officers' country should go into effect now. Looking around me, I see most of the men asleep now or about to doze off.

Everything about you I hold very dear to me and always will. I love you with all my heart. Every spare moment (and those that aren't spare) are taken up with thoughts of you. Good night, darling. I, too, am praying each night that God will grant us our chance to be together again and that I may do my job here to the best of my ability, because of you and because of what we're fighting for—peace on earth.

Author's Note: The sergeants are wondering, I'm sure, whether I have the stuff to make it in combat.

January 20, 1945

𝒟ear Ginny,

My three sergeant squad leaders just left the tent. It's the first time they've been over. It is a custom for the officer in charge to invite his squad leaders over for a drink every so often. After inviting them, I found the ice had run out. I even picked some limes for the occasion. They're really dandy men and have seen a lot of action on Cape Gloucester and Peleliu. So we spent a couple of hours in talk, they doing the most of it with their stories. Not that they care to brag about their infantry experiences, but having a new face to talk to seems to please them. They've been in the South Pacific area for over twenty months, so I can see why. Their attitude and spirit are not daunted by the fact that a man can be in just so much action before the law of averages catches up. They claim, however, that "the law of averages has been repealed, and if you're going to get it, you're going to get it." To my mind, this is a good way of looking at it. This doesn't mean, however, that you should stick your nose out of a foxhole for some fresh air while playing solitaire.

I can't help expressing almost all my feelings, especially about you and how my thoughts are always with you in everything I do and in my prayers at night. I keep saying the same things over and over, darling, because I mean them so very much. Waltz music and the old familiar tunes of peacetime are being played over the radio. I can hear them very clearly, and they remind me of soft, sweet-smelling summers and a carnival of laughter and silent moments of rest undisturbed except by happy expectations and contentment. All the things I wish for, the things I'm working every day for can be summed up in one desire: the chance to return to you, Ginny. Better close for now. I'm going to be exceptionally busy these next two weeks. Hope it won't interfere too much in writing to you. Possibly it will, so don't worry. Remember, you have all my love, always.

ॐ

Author's Note: Do people realize what kind of men it takes to win this war?

January 22, 1945

𝒟ear Ginny,

There is a story that is touching and exemplifies the spirit of these men. In Peleliu, a rifleman was wounded quite badly, shot through the chest. He was lying next to a cliff that was about forty feet off the ground. His buddy, seeing his condition, shouted for him to lie still and wait for help. The wounded man, knowing that his buddy would also be shot by attempting to rescue him, replied: "If you do, I'll throw myself over the cliff. I'm practically a goner. Go back." His buddy, ignoring the threat, started out. The wounded man then rolled himself over the cliff.

Your mail has been coming in fine shape, Ginny. So far I've gotten ten letters from you. They are ten of the most wonderful letters a guy could ask for. And I thank you so much for them. Yesterday I received one dated the tenth of January, which is mighty good service and the envy of the other officers. Their letters seem to date far back in December. We must have the mailman on our side. He is a good one to have helping us.

This is our first Sunday off in a long time. I just returned from a movie, which is an occasional treat. I am supposed to be preparing a lecture now on chemical warfare. But first I am going to let my thoughts wander to Sundays back home—Sundays with home-cooked meals and wishing we were riding together. I've seen several wild horses on the other islands. Felt like jumping on the back of one of them but didn't.

I'd better get to work. You must know, Ginny, how much you mean to me, how much I enjoy talking with you like this. It's all I look forward to.

ᘓ

January 25, 1945

Dear Mother & Dad,
Just a note tonight. Seems like my free time is taken up cen-
soring letters that the guys write and preparing lectures.

Lately we've been here at the main base holding infantry school, talking about everything from the function of the gas mask to how long it takes to dig a foxhole – so we can plan our time accordingly....

Thinking about the farm, right now. I'm thinking that when I return, I doubt I'll go off the farm, content to milk the cows and pitch hay for board and room. Pitching a little woo, also, with a certain girl across the way...

War news is encouraging in Europe....

Will be real busy for the next few weeks, so don't worry if you find an absence of letters....Love.

ᔓ

January 26, 1945

𝒟ear Ginny,

I'm almost in top physical shape. In a few more days I'll be the equal of some of the sergeants. These fellow are all muscle and can go for days at a time without sleep, or so it seems. Must end now. Taps and lights out.

ᔓ

February 1, 1945

𝒟ear Ginny,

I arm wrestled with my sergeants today. Won my share. I think the men respect me now for my strength as well as for my brains. When we get into combat, it'll help if they trust me 100%.

ॐ

Author's Note: On some of the islands in the jungle, the grass was taller than we were. We had to hack our way with machetes.

February 8, 1945

𝒟ear Ginny,

Lately we've been spending time where we have more appropriate terrain to train on. We returned last night much in the need of showers and hot food. Our experience during the last two weeks held all the glamour and color of the true South Pacific. First came the tropical, heat-induced sweating, then the cold rains, then sleeping on lizard-infested ground first in the moonlight, then with the eventual rain clouds coming to make you shiver beneath a soaking poncho. We had only rations. I have my own special recipe for these. Taking either the beans, stew, or hash, I drain the ration-tasting juice off and add water from my canteen, stir well, then add a few wild hot peppers and cook over sand or dirt that is mixed with gasoline and ignited. It really tastes pretty good.

Saw a good deal of the natives this time. Some speak English taught to them by missionaries in pre-war days, and I had several interesting conversations with a few of them.

They learned the English, but not too many of them kept the practice of Christianity.

Tonight we had quite a party in the club tent due to the excess liquor ration that accumulated while we were away. I lost a little bit at poker. There certainly is a fraternal spirit among the officers here. Lieutenant Deland, with whom I share this tent, went to Yale and lives in Scarsdale, New York. And don't forget that Scotty, whom I told you about, is in the next tent. Bill Terry is in reconnaissance, which was bivouacked across from us while we were away. We got together often, and one night had fun telling everyone about our old Ford at Camp Pendleton.

When I returned last night—tired, hungry, and dirty— all was forgotten when I saw six letters waiting for me. Each was filled with all your goodness, so thoughtful and sincere, so lovable with mutual thoughts. There was a thrill, extra heartbeats, and a smile of loving comfort that I had never experienced before. I read them many times, darling, and I love you so dearly for every word of passion. The yearning to be with you is so strong, I'll do my best—anything in order to return to you. Those dreams of the future become more beautiful than ever.

ॐ

February 8, 1945

Dear Mother & Dad,
We've been away for about ten days on one of the more prim-

itive areas in order to train in more appropriate terrain. So I'm back at our base finding several letters from you. Letters are certainly a comfort after I sweat under the tropical sun and after I shiver from nights in the rain. But it's all been very exciting....

Your trip to New York City, mother, ought to suit you well after several cold winter months. Ginny's mother should be pleasant company. Hopefully, you'll have a chance to see Ginny. Received a number of her letters, all very sincere and common sensed. Her letters help me a good bit.

Although, to tell the truth, everything amongst the officers is so fraternal and good natured and the work is so interesting, that I really haven't gotten to the stage where absence of women bothers me too much. We have our fun kidding each other about our colleges, singing, playing cards, and enjoying a drink during our spare time. However, there are times I wish I could snuggle up with Ginny. And I know the eventual frustration will catch up to me, although I'm fairly content now. Man can only be that way so long, nevertheless....

Will close for now.....Love.

February 9, 1945

Dear Ginny,

I'm officer of the day for today through tomorrow. In a few minutes I must inspect the sentries. I took this opportunity while on "easy" duty to censor the mail. At last I'm caught up.

I just brought into the tent a good cool drink of whiskey, water, and lime. Then I lit up a cigarette and decided to devote this time to "my girl back home." All day I look forward to these moments with you, Ginny. I sort of drift back to you and all our pleasant memories and the thrill that shall be ours when we're together again. Music is coming in clear tonight over the South Pacific network. I'm hearing all of the old songs along with some classical music. I've never felt happier since that last day we spent together. I feel so comfortable with your love and hopes, knowing that we are praying for each other each night. I'm sort of floating away on an imaginary magic carpet bound for you and all of the things we could do together. I think of eating home-cooked food, enjoying the snow, or the beauty of the summer while riding in the fields. So, I'll close for now my darling. It's time for me to inspect those sentries, and I know the sergeant of the guard is waiting for me to show up.

చ

Author's Note: Memories and friends become dearer and dearer.

February 11, 1945

$\mathcal{D}$ear Ginny,

Just a page or two tonight, darling. It's pretty late. Bill Terry and Norm White, along with Scotty, were in the tent tonight. We had several drinks, discussing everything from our future infantry operation to the old ninth grade days. Scott, quite high, just told his captain that it would be impossible to do any work tomorrow, because he was having such a good time tonight. He is a great talker, and he has an array of coal mining stories that would make history if printed. Scotty says a lot of coal miners wouldn't work in any other job, because when they're underground they can't get hit by lightning. I'm not quite sure I believe him.

I've missed you terribly of late, Ginny. No mail has been coming through, which makes it worse. Your letters control my happiness, and without them, I'm blue. But I re-read the others, and the thrill is always as new as the first time.

Better close now, Ginny. Everyone is in bed, and I imagine this light is keeping some of the fellows awake. But I had to write you. Good night, darling. You'll be in my prayers and in my every thought.

ॐ

February 12, 1945

$\mathcal{D}$ear Ginny,

Another page or two tonight, darling. Just returned from seeing *Marriage Is A Private Affair*. I imagine it was a good picture in the eyes of the theater critics, but Lana Turner became so obnoxious with her uncertainty about love that I felt uncomfortable throughout the show. She considered love so complicated and complex—fed by mere animal instincts. And when that dies out at the slightest inclination, there is nothing left but the prospect of a thrill for something new. Why shouldn't it be as simple as it's made to be? It's a beautiful, contented, comfortable, doubtless feeling. One should know it if it's there and be unafraid of its consequences. So speaks a young man with probably lots to learn, but firm with his present convictions about love and war.

I miss you, darling, and I want you as always. I'll cherish every word of your letters, knowing the thoughts behind them came from one who is sincere, pure, natural, unaffected, and beautiful.

৵

February 13, 1945

*D*ear Ginny,

Not much to do here after a hard day of training except eat, drink, and sleep. I'm so used to the hard field work now, that it's difficult for me to get tired. A short shot of whiskey or bourbon kills the tension, the tension that's always there, right under the surface, waiting to play mind games with us.

৵

February 18, 1945

$\mathcal{D}$ear Ginny,

Thank you for your Valentine and birthday greetings. I'll always be your Valentine as you will always be mine.

Real short on time, darling. Hope my letters start coming to you soon. There will be a few days now that I'll be unable to write. But don't worry, I can take care of myself.

༅

February 21, 1945

$\mathcal{D}$ear Ginny,

I got a letter from my brother, Dick. Most of it had been censored. If you talk with my mom, tell her he's O.K. He probably doesn't write as much as I do. We had a freak storm two days ago. We're still repairing tents and cleaning fallen tree parts. At least it's something different for a change.

༅

February 24, 1945

$\mathcal{D}$ear Mother & Dad,

Another day in the South Pacific and everything about the same. Received a very nice letter from Dick the other day and just finished writing him with congratulations on his rating of corporal.

Pavuvu, South Pacific

Hope you enjoyed yourself in New York City, mother. Were you able to see Ginny? And, dad, I trust you got along all right by yourself.

Bill Terry and I have been together most of the evenings. We see a show, sitting on our buckets and converse over a couple of beers until bedtime. Once in a while Norm White joins us. His wife Betty may call you.

We're getting itchy to be on our way. I'm feeling fine and happy, only lonely and restless…. Ginny has been writing some very nice letters.

Remember to follow the First Marine Division. Perhaps you'll worry later on, but remember I'm well trained and that all my foxholes will be good and deep…. Love.

ॐ

February 26, 1945

Dear Ginny,

Norm White joined us at the club tent three nights ago, and we had fun remembering the old days together.

I have my 45-caliber pistol now, which is my pet. I clean all the parts and work the holster with saddle soap. I still have my carbine, too. I received some binoculars the other day that are seven power (100 yards at 700 yards). I made a canvas case for my radio, which I can attach to my pack. So, I'm pretty well fixed.

It's Sunday night. One of the fellows is playing some records. Soon the radio will bring us the same Sunday night radio programs transcribed at the time we would hear them as if we were home. We'll get Jack Benny, Charley McCarthy, and The Hour of Charm. It's practically impossible to feel so far away on Sunday night. If it were a Sunday night at home, though, maybe we'd be relaxing, tired from a day of skiing. That's the picture I'm out here for. There are lots of things I'm unable to tell you, darling. And if my letters now begin to be farther apart, please don't worry. My heart will always be with you, Ginny, loving you each moment, needing your nearness, and dreaming of being together with you. You must know, my darling, how much you mean to me and how dearly I love you and all the wonderfulness you stand for. Knowing that we are both keeping faith and trust in each other and that God's watching over us gives me all the spirit necessary. Please don't worry. Every part of me says all my love, always.

ک۲

March 2, 1945

*D*ear Ginny,

Some things I just can't tell you about in my letters, Ginny. Censorship is important to troop safety. I've been briefed on our mission, and it's not going to be an easy job for me and the fellows. We know definitely now that we'll be leaving in about a week. I'll write whenever I can, and I'll hope the letters get through to you as quickly as possible. Keep praying.

Part 4

Aboard A Landing Ship Tank
March 1945 — April 1945

March 9, 1945

Dear Ginny,

Another night. But this time, Ginny, I'm aboard ship, and the water is dotted with dimly lighted ships all around us in shimmering seas. There is some excitement, but most of us are subdued.

This is the start of the object of all our training. We're finally off to war. It's a chance really to do our part.

Thought I'd have time to write a longer letter, but I've got to leave you now. Believe me, darling, coming back to you is the plot of all my dreams and delightful expectations. Loving you is the most powerful, everlasting thing that has ever happened to me.

ॐ

March 13, 1945

To Ginny:

> *I'm at a place I know not where*
> *It's dark, the water's rough*
>
> *Dreariness of life makes me as Poe*
> *Deep in solitude, creatures dark and low*
>
> *Byron brings out brave spirit of love*
> *Made in the heavens above*
>
> *Then I become gallant as Tennyson has said*
> *Afraid of no one, even the dead*
>
> *Edward Guest brings me back home*
> *Then suddenly I'm no longer alone*

Walking in the countryside with Whittier
Makes life a good bit prettier

Longfellow brings back America of old
Stout-hearted men, true and bold

The dead I hear when Bryant speaks
In and out of graves it sneaks

Mountain slopes along with Shelly
Woods, flowers, roses, lilies

Keats makes meager food seem good
Charcoaled, flavored o'er with fragrant wood

Thoughts of the night on rolling seas
Harry

ᔕ

March 19, 1945

Dear Mother & Dad,
I'm at a place I know not where. It's dark, and the water is
rough. I'm not allowed to tell you anything specific. And,
I'm sorry for the long delay. I'm in a situation where no mail
can be sent or received, so have missed hearing from you. It
seems like such a long time.

Imagine the snow is fading away now and the grass
beginning to show. Easter isn't far away. Two more days,
and spring will begin. The farm will seem more alive now.
You might want to see how the cabin withstood the winter.

Words are scarce tonight. Possibly you thought I was on

Aboard A Landing Ship Tank

Iwo Jima. It was quite a tough operation for the Marine Corps. Victory came dearly.

Though my letters may be far between from now on, please don't worry. I have strong faith and trust that we'll all be home together again soon....Love.

ॐ

March 25, 1945

𝒟ear Ginny,

Sorry for the long delay, Ginny. And there may be yet a longer delay. I'd like to say things of interest about my daily duties, but you know I can't. With no mail for such a long time (I've lost count), I miss you more than ever. I just checked your last letter, and it's been over a month since anything was delivered to me. I feel farther away than ever. I guess I'm not complaining, because much of what I do on our ship is interesting and exciting. But everything civilized is unfortunately, so very far away. I imagine you are planning to celebrate Easter at home.

With March upon us, I can see the blossoming of spring back home. Buds are no doubt showing on the trees and bushes, and there's probably an inkling of green in the grass. The scent of dry, dead winter is being driven away by the scent of warmth and the new arousing of nature. On the Hudson, the ice cakes will be rushing, with a March wind driving them down the river. And soon, the ice will disappear, leaving the banks free to the sun, and the water will become quiet, with a hint of blue shining brightly. In Millbrook, the gardens will be attended to, and the stone bridge will be frequented by the strolling populace in their new spring clothes. The girls will wear smart new suits, while the men will have smooth cut topcoats and felt hats. No one will have to wear galoshes or turned up collars. The slush will be gone, the walks clean and dry. I know the lingering of winter, but the best is not so far away. Tonight, I'm in tune with the seasons.

I certainly have gone off on a tangent, darling. It's only because you make me want all those things. Good night, Ginny. Thanks for your prayers. You are never left out of mine.

ॐ

March 27, 1945

Dear Ginny,

We must be getting where we are going, since we have been briefed on what we are going to do.

One meeting was about the Japanese language where we were taught to say such things as "come on out, we won't hurt you." The island where we are going is filled with many caves, and we can use that phrase when we are flushing them out. We want prisoners so we can interrogate them. Also, it was explained that we have to be careful about the Japanese tricking us with our own language. They are taught to say some of our first names. So, if they yell, "Hey, Jack," and there is a Jack nearby, Jack may answer by standing up. Or, by simply answering, he will become a target. Our corpsmen have been warned that they may call out "Corpsman, I'm hit." If the corpsman comes running to give aid, he's a target, too.

I was explaining to my platoon at a meeting that the Japanese have difficulty in pronouncing the letter "L," but they can say the letter "H" quite well. And, while we have enjoyed a real familiar relationship throughout our training by the men calling me Harry, I'd appreciate it, that from now on, if they would call me Lang, no more Harry. Then, someone in the back shouted, "O.K., Harry."

I know who it was, my machine gun sergeant who has combat experience. Also, he is older than most of us. While he has been very cooperative during training, he and another experienced sergeant have me on a "let's wait and see how I do in combat" attitude.

There is no doubt I'll be tested. By the whole platoon. I'm willing to accept that. After all these months of training, from boot camp, back in October of 1943, to this point, all I've done is to train myself as a rifle platoon leader. This has given me the confidence I needed. I feel the men trust me. Trust, to them, is that I know what I'm doing.

Trust to you and me, Ginny, well, we know all about trust, trusting in the faith that will carry us through. I've got a real good feeling about that. And a most wonderful feeling about you, my darling.

ॐ

March 29, 1945

Dear Mother & Dad,
With great surprise today, I received mail from you and
Ginny. After such a long time without mail, my morale was
certainly boosted by your letters and the pictures. The pic-
ture of Dick is especially good. Can hardly believe he weighs
191 now. Tell him I'll bet it's 50% beer and 50% chocolate
cake.

  Glad you had such a good time in New York City. Your
description of Ginny was, shall I say, endearing. She sure is
the object of my affection.... Your birthday cake didn't make
it. I'll enjoy it when it does....

  Everything around here is about the same. You know there
is little I'm allowed to say. So, good night for now and don't
worry....Love.

ॐ

Author's Note: We have been picked to be in the first assault
wave. Because of a sea wall guarding the beach, we will be
carrying ladders.

April 1, 1945

Dear Ginny,
I'm up on the deck. It's 2:00 A.M. It's Easter Sunday.
Somewhere out there is the island we are going to land on
this morning. The day we have been training for. In the belly

of the ship are the landing craft that we will board to take us in. I couldn't explain that earlier because of the censorship. The front of this LST opens up like a giant garage door to let us out onto the water, probably a good distance from shore.

I'm up here by myself. The rest of the troops will be getting up at 3:00 A.M. And I'm looking at the stars, a mass of them, and thinking that while growing up, little did I know I'd be here in the Pacific Ocean thousands of miles from home, in combat gear, wondering whether I am scared or just nervous. I've got it figured that being just a little scared is O.K., because it will make me cautious. And, Ginny, we are so highly trained, be assured we will be victorious. So, please don't worry.

It's a beautiful night. The soft, fresh breeze of spring. I'm really quite tranquil. The ship is gently rolling along very slowly, moving into position.

From our letters we know about our dreams. We are now rounding the bend to take me home to live those dreams. All my love, forever.

Part 5

Battle Of Okinawa
April 1945 — June 1945

Okinawa is part of the Ryukyu Islands close to Japan; the original Allied plan was to use Okinawa as a jumping off point for a full-scale invasion of Japan.

ॐ

April 20, 1945

Dear Ginny,

Possibly you've guessed I'm on Okinawa; it's cold in the fox-holes at night. Our invasion has probably been in the news back home. I'm writing with a Jap pen, Jap ink, and Jap paper. This is all that is available. Generally, I've tried to stay away from Japanese equipment as much as possible. It has a certain feel and aroma that I've learned to hate.

Some of the experiences have been very interesting so far, while others I'll always try to forget forever—like see-ing somebody die you knew well in life. You feel sorry, but, deep in your subconscious, you thank God that it's not you.

The island itself in landscape and culture is as a geogra-phy book would describe it—typically Japan. Except for the enemy, it is very beautiful. The weather is much like that in California.

I'm keeping with the faith that is so strong between us, Ginny. And I yearn for your yearnings as well. Some day it will all come true and will be as beautiful as our dreams. It's hard to write much at the present. We never get any warn-ing about protecting ourselves from attack. I can say that our invasion force is making progress. Will try to write with each opportunity.

ॐ

April 20, 1945

Dear Mother & Dad,

A note to insure you I'm as fine as you can expect. You've probably guessed that I'm on Okinawa now writing to you with a Jap pen and Jap paper. They're the only writing tools available at present.

Yes, I have been receiving your mail. Mail is a high priority here and is delivered straight to the lines with the ammunition and rations. Glad you're both well and the farm growing so well under the influence of spring....

The weather so far is ideal with the exception of a very cold foxhole at night. I've had some very interesting experiences and, of course, some that I'm willing to forget forever. I've had a three-week beard. Our new K rations are filling, and I have no thirst — except for beer and milk. Haven't seen Norm White or Bill Terry yet.

My strong faith tells me the Lang family will be home together before long.....Love.

ॐ

April 24, 1945

Dear Ginny,

We came into this small village on the coast. That means there are no Japs on one side of us, the ocean. That's good for a change. This is our first contact with the Okinawa people who wander about trying to scratch it out with whatever is left.

In reality there are no rules of war. Not when it's being fought. Anything goes. And that's what happened yesterday when a group of these people, children, women and old men moved towards us along a wide roadway. I didn't pay much attention at first and then, I don't know, I became a little suspicious. The looks on those people's faces seemed strange. But then how would I know about these people?

Then from behind them, hand grenades were flying at us, fortunately falling short. We moved into the brush cover on each side of the road and worked our way towards the group—and then the people started screaming, thinking we were after them. My guess now was that the Japs were using these people as a shield. What we were trying to do was to get to the back of the column for a look. Sure enough, there were two Japs with their bayonets forcing these people forward. We didn't have a clear shot at them without a stray shot hitting the civilians. When they spotted us, they threw down their weapons and fell to the ground. That solved the problem. Now we have two prisoners, apparently beat up strays, on their way now to our headquarters, which is too good of a fate for them. And we are worse off, because I had to give up two of our guys to escort them.

And so it goes. Anyway, we are back in the hills, stopping for what we loosely call lunch—cold K rations as usual. But this gives me a chance to write.

One of your letters arrived two days ago. Sounds like you

had a great time with your mother on her visit to your school. Spring along the Hudson River sounds so good. Your snapshot is in my bible. You are with me every moment.

⤳

Author's Note: We were unable to change dungarees, even though lice have infested the seams. Because most of the fighting is at night, and we can't move for fear of detection, we don't scratch. Mail is brought to us along with the ammunition. While listening to my radio, I intercepted the conversation of two pilots up above saying that President Roosevelt had died—like many of us.

April 28, 1945

𝒟ear Ginny,

Another chance to write, finally. It has now been 28 days in the front lines for me. I haven't had a chance to take a bath yet, as we're living in our foxholes. The last few days have been relatively peaceful. After searching for some paper and a pen, I have found a box to use as a writing table and have pulled it into the shade of a small pine tree. This is the first chance I've had to relax since landing in the first wave. But tonight the enemy will be up in our lines, sneaking around our foxholes, and coming at us from the air as usual with their artillery. It's true what I heard before about the Japanese. There really are suicide soldiers. These fanatics have jumped into some of our foxholes.

There is no rest at night. I have only half of my original platoon left now. Some died, and some were wounded and are now on their way to a hospital. So you can see, Ginny, that Okinawa is not as easy as the press may say, because of a sort of easy landing. I've become so primitive as far as living conditions are concerned, that I'll probably have to learn civilization all over again—like eating off a plate, sleeping on a bed, or tying a tie. But it will be fun re-learning.

Every few days I have a letter from you, darling. And your letters are so wonderful that without them under these conditions I wonder if I'd stay sane. As it is, I'm relaxed, dreaming of how it would be to enjoy your closeness now, thinking of what we would do together. It may be a long time before that happens, but someday we'll be together doing what we've dreamed about. And all of what we'll do will have the color and the beauty it deserves. I can feel it will happen, Ginny. Before long I'll tell you what fighting for every inch of ground is about. But not now. So, I'll close, my darling. Keep the faith of our love and God.

୬

April 28, 1945

Dear Mother & Dad,
Another opportunity to write. Just finished cleaning my carbine and shaved this morning for the first time in 28 days. Still haven't bathed, and I've taken my shoes off only twice – to change socks. Nevertheless, I feel half clean.

We're still on the front lines, living in foxholes. The Japs have stopped coming at us for the time being, except at night. Being alert at night has made us all tired, and my platoon needs a rest and a chance to clean up. Of my original platoon, exactly half of us are left. Our medical reports say the wounded are doing fine; some fellows are even back in the states.....

Let's hope the war ends soon....Love.

༄

May 8, 1945

Dear Ginny,

Coming in here, I thought I was well briefed on combat. I find now that one of the things you have to do is to fight not only the enemy but you have to fight off a lot of anguish. Each day I have to go to the company command post to be briefed on our next move and to report the names of the dead and wounded in my platoon. Depending on what's happening, I can't make it every day. Anyway, this reporting casualties is treated stoically, just like the business of the day. The Captain says nothing. I say nothing. The rest of the guys in the command post say nothing. You'd think we'd say something like "too bad about so and so." Even when there are no casualties to report you'd think there might be an expression of pleasure. No. We have trained ourselves to dismiss these emotions almost immediately, so we can concentrate solely on the tactics at hand. We cannot be distracted.

In every advance some men must be the point. That is, they go first, to find the best route and to scout enemy positions. Unfortunately, they are the first to draw enemy fire. Assigning these men to that position is real tough. Our guys never quiver at the assignment. But I do. They don't know that.

There are times within the platoon that we chat about home, loved ones, real food, things like that. As a matter of fact these are the most cherished moments. And we get to know each other like brothers. And, most certainly, we express our feelings about losing one of us.

Many know about you, Ginny. After this is over, we're going to keep contact, and they will be wondering what happened to Ginny and Lang, as they call me, and we will be telling them how great it is. You just wait and see, my darling.

ॐ

Author's Note: Sergeant Bishop's wristwatch was eventually lost, dammit.

May 10, 1945

Dear Ginny,

I've got to talk to you about friendship, deep friendship among us. From all the days of training together, to fighting together. The number two guy in my platoon is the Platoon Sergeant. He and I share a foxhole. We each sleep an hour at a time when we can. Each protects the other. How close can you get to a guy?

Well now I'm alone. Bishop was shot this afternoon, a bullet piercing his eyes. He is alive and will survive without sight. Our company was moving through a heavily wooded, hilly area when we heard the jibber-jabber of Japs talking rather loudly. Assuming they were distracted and we were not detected, one platoon was sent up a ridge, with my platoon following. Suddenly, that ridge was bombarded with everything. They had us zeroed in. Bishop and I were caught in an open space on the ridge and were racing for cover when he was shot. Even with his wound, he kept going until we fell next to a small mound that shielded us, and then we crawled until we reached some of the platoon. We stayed on the ground to catch our breath when Bishop reached down to his wrist and took off his watch, put his arm around me with a hug and said, "Here, Lang, I want you to have my watch. I won't be needing it anymore." My arm went around him. I guess I sobbed.

This happened on top of everything else yesterday, when we also lost Mac, my faithful, trusty runner, the guy that stuck by my side, delivering my messages. From time to time he also carried my hand-held radio that we called the Spam Can. He went off to pass the word to one of my squads and was shot by a sniper. One lousy, lucky shot. He would have shared my foxhole with Bishop gone. I still yell for Mac when I want something done.

I have to fight sadness quickly. Have to stay focused every minute. This job doesn't allow time to grieve. When this war is over, I'm going to properly grieve for all my guys lost, for the rest of my life.

Why am I telling you all this, Ginny? I don't usually tell you about such things. I don't want you to live the horrors of war.

I'm going to stop right here.

∂

Author's Note: If I had the choice of a bath for this stinking body or an hour of silence with no gunfire, I'd take the silence.

May 16, 1945

𝒟ear Ginny,

I'm still on the front lines, unbathed and unshaven, with a moment's rest from the enemy, deep in a foxhole. The Japs are not far away now. Sniper bullets are starting to zoom overhead, and shells are starting to fall. I'm dirty and tired, always cautious of an enemy soldier sneaking up behind me. Each day now for 46 days it's been almost the same. We've seen an unusual amount of action. Each advance we make brings on more of the enemy. Just after V.E. day in the States, we were attacking ridge number so and so. This was quite ironical, considering the celebration back home. Hope the people don't relax or lay down on their jobs with the European Theatre Operations over with now. The Japs won't surrender. They must be killed. All I can say about conditions here is that out of my 54 men I arrived with there are only 14 of us left. I guess numbers speak for themselves.

After all that I've been through, it's almost impossible for you to imagine what it is like to receive your precious words. I pray each spare moment for peace and for the chance to be home and with you again, darling. So let's forget this damn island now. I want to say I do love you dearly. You are beside me. The spirit of you, home, and God is what gives me my faith.

With the month of May, I can picture you at school, involved in all of your activities. Getting ready for graduation is quite a thrill, yet sentimentally disturbing. I'll bet you hate to leave in a way. I know I did when I was in college. There is something everlasting about the alma mater and your friends. Mother wrote that she had seen some proofs of your graduation pictures, and they were dandy. I sure would like to have one. Just a reminder to you that we're not allowed to receive any packages here, just letters. With me, I carry that snapshot of you sitting in the snow sled, and I look at it each chance I get. Best of luck and congratulations on your graduation. In the future, we'll take a trip back east and see both of our schools again. I have to close for now, darling. Please don't worry about me. We'll be together, someday soon.

May 16, 1945

Dear Mother & Dad,

Yesterday I received a letter from you acknowledging the letter I wrote from here. Am awfully glad you received it, for I'm sure it eased your mind somewhat.

I'm really fed up with fighting. I'm still on the front line in a foxhole, unbathed. Forty six days without a bath or hot food does try a man. I've seen an exceptionally large amount of action lately. And there seem to be more Japs as we advance. Nevertheless, we're doing well. I really think we're not far from saying the worst is over with.

When I return home, I'm going to appreciate everything from emptying the garbage to getting up early. And how I can smell your cooking, mother! Some homemade cake and cookies, salad, soup, pot roast, milk. I can actually taste it now. And I'm going to see an awfully lot of Ginny, too.

That's about all for now, folks. Will write again soon and be sure not to worry....Love.

༜

May 23, 1945

Dear Ginny,

Just a page or so while sitting in what I'd call a deluxe fox-hole. We've dug into the side of a hill and put a pup tent over it. We've spread a poncho and a blanket on the sand inside, which makes us rather comfortable. We're free from the rain and wind outside. At present, we're in back of the front lines resting for a day or two before going back up. It's strange not to hear the whizzing of bullets or the bursting of shells. The men had to have a rest and a chance for some sleep—though all of us are still alert for any sneaking enemy soldiers.

Your letters, darling, have been coming quite frequently—and as ever they bring me back to feeling human again. They make me warm inside and give me peace—especially after those times when the going has been really rough. Each letter makes us closer together. Hope you enjoyed your trip to Atlantic City and that your graduation was nice. I love you.

჻

May 23, 1945

Dear Mother & Dad,

Just a page this time to say again I'm in good health and still kicking around on this island. At present, we are resting behind the lines, which is a rare and delightful treat. Still minus hot water, hot chow, and showers; but the absence of whizzing bullets and bursting shells makes life a luxury. I've practically a new platoon now. Very few of the originals are left — 13 out of 54.

Your letters have been arriving frequently. I want to offer best wishes on your 25th anniversary. Hope I am as successful with marriage as you two have been. Also glad to know

Dick has been assigned to an aircraft carrier as part of a Marine unit. Should be good duty.... Ginny's letters are very enlightening to my morale. Naturally, they remind me of my frustrations.

The situation here looks better each day, and we should secure the entire island soon. Most of the boys have plenty of souvenirs. The only souvenir I want is myself....Love.

꒜

Author's Note: Bill Terry was wounded on this mission.

June 1, 1945

𝒟ear Ginny,

Now it is exactly two months since we landed. Each night has been spent in a foxhole, the last five nights in very wet ones, for it has been raining constantly, and we have no shelter. Helmets are our umbrellas, and ponchos protect our shoulders and keep our weapons partially dry. The seat of my dungarees has been constantly wet. Last night while sitting in a foxhole half-filled with water, and while holding the phone (connected to the company command post), lightning struck the line and blew the thing right out of my hand. At the same time I was burning up with what I thought was a high fever. In the morning I asked the corpsman to take my temperature. You know what? It was normal.

We are now in a holding position on the bank of a river we are preparing to cross. It is only about fifty yards wide, shallow, with boulders scattered about. I think we can hop across on those boulders. There is enough of a let-up in the rain now so I can write. But what I want to tell you is, that of all the guys I was hoping to see, Bill Terry with his reconnaissance platoon came through our lines and crossed the river into enemy territory to get the lowdown on what lies ahead for us. We could only speak briefly. Then he had to get sentimental, saying, "wonder what happened to Baby." He was making reference to what we called our old Ford car back at Camp Pendleton. I might see him on his way back when he reports to intelligence. How great it was to see him.

And do you know what else is great, Ginny? We are about to push those Japs right off the end of this island. It's getting that close. Even with this skeleton platoon, fatigued as we are, our spirits are high in that anticipation.

No letters for awhile with this rain slowing things down. But your letters are one thing that is dry in my backpack. Just having those letters close to me means you are with me night and day. Now if I can just get my butt dry. All my love.

ॐ

Author's Note: If you go to sleep, you may wake up dead.

June 5, 1945

Dear Ginny,
The first light of dawn means I've faced the worst of it. Now comes the easy part. Easy means I can stand up. It gets

cramped in a foxhole. And, secondly, I can now attend to my private matters instead of urinating in my helmet and pouring it out. Nobody gets out of a foxhole at night.

The worst of it means that often the Japs try to retake our positions. It usually starts at midnight. Since dark they have been silently working their way towards us. Some of them have piano wire attached to a piece of wood at each end, to wrap around your neck. Throwing hand grenades in your foxhole is a favorite. You'd better throw them back before they explode. And they shout at us. Why do they do that? Often the leader will stand up, waving his sword, calling for his men to move as a group.

All this time our people in the rear are firing flares that light up the sky in an eerie light, making everything appear as a silhouette. One flare after another, all night. How many nights have I had like this? I don't know.

Several times now when we go into the second night without sleep, I experience periods of hallucinations. Bushes and trees take on the form of a moving person. I can't be sure of anything. So I throw needless hand grenades and fire my weapon just to be sure.

That's careless. I've got to get those hallucinations under control.

The Japs are getting more fanatical as they run out of turf, and they know we've learned their tricks.

Won't be long now, Ginny. Intelligence tells us that at the end of the island they are already jumping off the cliffs, in disgrace.

Author's Note: We are on the outskirts of the village of Itoman on the coast of the China Sea in a demolished pigsty. My depleted platoon is taking a barrage of small arms fire. The ground is too rocky to dig, so we are rushing to pile up broken pieces of block from the pigsty to get some cover. While moving one of the blocks with my shovel, I see a hand grenade thrown at me. It knocks me flat, leaving me disoriented and bleeding through the bowels from the blast. However, I have miraculously escaped the shrapnel. All the weapons of our platoon begin firing to resist the attack long enough for two of the men to carry me to the nearby sea wall, while still being sniped at. Fortunately, our radio is still working, and the radio man is able to contact a ship that soon dispatches an amphibious landing craft. I am picked up by my buddies and thrown over the sea wall to the sand below, left to wait for the landing craft, secure from the snipers. The next thing I know, I am on sheets with the gentle hands of a nurse rubbing my back, her aroma making me believe that I had died and gone to heaven.

Part 6

Aboard A Hospital Ship
June 1945

June 12, 1945

𝒟ear Ginny,

I'm on a hospital ship. Technically, I'm listed as wounded in action. But don't worry, I'm all right. I'm a victim of blast concussion (shell shock). It was hard to take. Now I am recovering fast with only an aching and hazy head. Actually, it didn't happen all at once now that I am able to remember more clearly. I had a slight case of it for quite awhile. Several times the concussion from the shell blasts took my helmet right off. And if I had the chin strap fastened, I suffered a real jolt. This time, the mortar and the grenade blasts were too much. So I'm real lucky. But I hated to leave the men. I only had ten left, including three originals that I landed with. All day long I was lying here wondering about them and what they were doing. From what little we know, there didn't appear to be much fighting left to do. I spent seventy foxhole days fighting, shooting and getting shot at. So I feel somewhat content with the thought that I've accomplished something.

This life now is a dream. I have white sheets, food on a plate, sleep. No worries about an enemy. It's hard to believe. I guess I proved that you can get used to hell.

I'm certainly proud of my outfit and the way we fought the last couple of weeks. We really had the Japs on the run. It's funny how all my talk always relates back to Okinawa. Each sunset brings on a restless night—with the fighting no doubt in my subconscious. Consciously, I sleep, but deep in my mind I'm on the defensive. I'm sure I'll outgrow this with time.

I was able to keep the things in my pack—the bible with your picture in it and some pictures of the farm. Also, I got to keep my faithful helmet, pistol, and knife. The bible has been a great blessing. My faith in the goodness of God is so strong now that it will never be broken under any circumstances. He certainly gave me comfort in battle, and I know that in peacetime He will also.

My daydreams are most pleasant. Fanciful they are. I pray they'll soon come true along with a world of peace. While here in bed all day, I'm often with you, darling. I picture you at home and what you are doing. Hope you drop around to the farm once in awhile to see mother and dad. They sure like you and are always eager to see you. I haven't gotten any mail in about three weeks—for we were pushing through the enemy lines quite fast, and the mail never did catch up.

To hold you tight is a precious dream. I think about riding the horses, sitting around the house thinking up things to do, maybe raise the devil somewhere. It's fun to think about. I have a feeling it won't be long now. I'll say good-night for this time. Say hello to your mother.

ॐ

June 12, 1945

Dear Mother & Dad,

I find myself minus weapon and foxhole. In place, is a clean white bed, nurses. Don't be alarmed, for nothing serious is wrong with me.

Though listed as wounded in action, I've not a scratch on

me except *flea bites and a few cuts. Diagnosis proves that I'm a victim of blast concussion. Guess I came too close, too many times to bursting shells and hand grenades. I stuck it out on the front lines, 70 foxholes. I sure hated to leave with fighting still to be done, but it should be over soon....*

At present, I'm on a hospital ship still in a harbor at Okinawa. Actually it feels as if I'm really in a first-class hospital. As far as I'm concerned, I'll never complain about another thing. And if I do, you be sure to remind me of the last 70 days. When the going was tough and we were in a tight spot, I'd look up into the sky, think of home – and pray. I've become a genuine Christian, and I'll never lose my faith in God.

It's a relief to write you. At first my memory was so bad, I couldn't remember a thing. I knew I had to write you, but I couldn't put my words down in writing, and I couldn't' remember your address. It's quite normal now, though hazy at times. So I'll close for now, folks....Love.

৲

Author's Note: Little did I realize the War Department had sent a telegram to mother and dad saying I was wounded in combat, leaving them worried about how badly.

June 15, 1945

*D*ear Ginny,

I keep hoping that my last letter about me being safe has

wings and gets to you in record time. I've written a similar letter to mother and dad.

My mind has moved, at the moment, away from thinking about my men, to realizing now what you and mother and dad have been going through since our landing on April 1. It's got to be like when a person you love goes into the hospital operating room and you are in the waiting room pacing the floor and waiting for the surgeon to come out, hoping for the best, but fearing the worst. Only this time, you were in the waiting room for months.

So, I visualize you opening that letter. I see your smile, hear your words of joy, rushing to tell your mother, calling my mother and dad and then wanting to be alone to revel in the sensation of happiness that sort of tingles through your body, and with closed eyes, your smile continues to conjure up what this letter really means.

When I visualize mother and dad, I see them embracing, tears of thankfulness trickling down their cheeks, both hoping that my brother Dick is safe as well.

Ginny, pray that wars will stop. Killing each other, wounding each other, the pain, the sacrifice, time taken out of our lives to fight wars, it's just so ungodly. But then, it did make a difference. I don't know. I hope so.

I'll be writing you from someplace soon. No one seems to know.

I feel so lucky to still have your snapshot, right here on this little table beside me along with your letters that are my main reading material. I'm so thankful and so in love. Good night, Ginny.

Part 7

Army Hospital On Saipan
June 1945 — July 1945

Saipan is in the Mariana Islands grouped with Guam and Tinian.

ॐ

June 17, 1945

𝒟ear Ginny,

Never thought I'd ever be talking to a Japanese girl. There is one beside my bed that just finished cleaning my table. She's really little. I may have embarrassed her with some of my Japanese lingo. She just laughs. I'm in an Army hospital on the island of Saipan. You'd be surprised at the number of nurses working on the island. These brave women do a commendable job and accept this South Pacific life without a complaint. One year ago yesterday the Marines landed on this beach.

It's a Sunday afternoon so peaceful and quiet with a distant radio playing somewhere. My only emotion is laziness, and my only passions are you and home. This is an afternoon I've longed for back when I was deep inside a wet foxhole. What's missing are your letters. It's been so long since the last one. But, Ginny, you are always deep in my heart, never to leave. Being here in such peace this afternoon, you seem closer to me than usual, darling. I have a feeling the war is almost over. Let's keep the faith. I'll close for now. Don't know where I'll go from here. Keep writing to my old address for now.

ॐ

June 17, 1945

Dear Mother & Dad,
Here I am on Saipan. I'm much better, with only headaches
and a cramped up stomach. I say "only," because if you
have to be wounded, this is a blessing. I'd been shot at and
missed so many times, the law of averages should have
caught me. Then when shells did hit next to me, I only
received the blast concussion. Early in that very last day a
Jap stuck his rifle practically in my face, fired and missed.
Almost simultaneously I fired at him and missed. We both
backed away. My aim was getting pretty bad. That's what
the Jap thought, too, I'm sure. Guess that's why we called it
a draw....

Today, I see is Father's Day, so the best to the best
father..... Love.

ॐ

June 20, 1945

Dear Ginny,
I feel pretty good tonight—extremely well for some reason.
Perhaps it's because I'm returning to my old self again. At
least memories of Okinawa aren't bothering me as much. I
can still hear the constant noise of the shelling, but the vol-
ume has gone down.

In our ward we have a radio, which seems to make a great difference with the patients. Saipan has a radio station that transcribes the programs we used to hear at home—and we hear them at the hours we were familiar with as well.

In a day or so I'll write a longer letter, darling. I've fooled around doing nothing today. Most all of the time I stayed in bed—it has been strange. So now it's time for the lights to go out. I have been thinking of you in such glorious detail today. Guess what occupied all of my time? I daydreamed that I was wearing the Marine dress uniform, campaign ribbons and all. You were wearing a formal gown, you had your hair done up, and you were wearing flowers. We were fit to knock 'em dead. We had dinner at a most lush place and had a nice, quiet, contented ride home in no particular hurry. I'll kiss you good-night now.

༄

June 21, 1945

Dear Mother & Dad,
Another line or so to insure you that I'm coming along fine. We've a radio in the ward with good music and the news on the hour. From what I hear, Okinawa is about finished.

We had a tough fighting outfit, folks, and I mean we could handle those Japs. The day before I left, our company made a 3,000-yard push with my platoon out in front. We advanced so fast the Japs didn't know which way to run.

Our objectives was the China Sea. We arrived there about 5:00 P.M. on a hill overlooking a wide coral rock road running along the coast. Along the road ran hundreds of soldiers and civilians. So we just sat there, picking off the soldiers like ducks, avoiding the civilians. Then suddenly, right in front of us about 50 yards away, we saw some Japs trying to escape from a small ravine. We crawled up, and as they reached the top, we'd fire and let them fall to the bottom of the hill. After that, we found there were too many to take care of, so I called our mortars, and they finished them off with their shells.

You've probably been reading now of how the Japs are surrendering or killing themselves. We captured a Jap military doctor. I asked him, in the best Japanese I could manage, to take care of the dozen or so civilians we had captured also. He replied with an "OK," gathering them all in a circle. Then he pulls the pin on a hand grenade, blowing himself and the civilians apart. You never know what the devil they're going to do next. Mainly, because they're not like human beings. I convince myself that killing them is like killing ugly, dirty rats in the cellar, except that they're more sneaky and haunted than rats. They live like animals in caves, unsanitary, flea bitten and real smelly. Usually, they're doped up with narcotics or sake (rice liquor). At night, they charge our positions yelling like insane, wild animals. I'll admit it can scare the hell out of you at night no matter how many times you've heard them, but they become easy targets.

Well, I've certainly talked enough about Japs. It's hard

to get them off my mind. Thought I might as well say a lit-
tle something rather than lay here thinking about it.

By the way, I've quite a mustache now. It's been growing
since March 31st, the day before we landed. Speaking of
landing, I might mention my platoon had the honor of being
in the first wave. Back to the mustache, at first it was
blonde, then red for quite some time. Now, it's tinted with
red but is mostly a dishwater blonde mingled with a slight-
ly darker shade. It's long enough to twist and bushy enough
to tickle my nose.

Will write again soon....Love.

༈

June 22, 1945

Dear Ginny,

I just finished dinner. Our dessert was vanilla ice cream (a
real treat). The radio is now playing after-dinner music. The
news that finally the Marines raised our flag on Okinawa,
claiming it is secured, is certainly good news here. It makes
me feel much better. An island 325 miles from Japan is a
great victory for us. To have the satisfaction that I helped
bring this about makes me content and proud. I'm sorry I
didn't last until the end of the fighting, but I didn't miss
much.

Today the doctor hypnotized me. It's quite an experience, as if floating on air. Tonight at 10 P.M. he is going to
put me to sleep. It's something quite inexplicable. In the bed

across from mine is a Marine who lost his voice because of blast concussion. Through the doctor's hypnosis, his voice has returned. My troubles seem to be nightmares and headaches. We'll see what the doctor can do about that. I try to cooperate with his method as much as I can. It is as if I drift away to oblivious relaxation.

This afternoon the doctor hypnotized me again—and this time I was absolutely, completely helpless. Before I went to sleep, he told me my right arm would rise in the air. And by gosh, after awhile, I found it to be just so. A ton of bricks couldn't pull my arm down unless he said so. Although I remember little of it, he asked me many questions about the time I was hit with the biggest blast. My memory about that particular incident is rather vague. He said, though, that my medical progress is quite pleasing. Evidently, I remembered something. Gradually, my medical condition is clearing up. As far as treatment is concerned, there isn't much to do except rest.

At present the wounded here in the ward who are able to get around are awaiting planes for the States. I certainly envy them. I doubt that my condition is serious enough to warrant much more than a rest for awhile. Mentally, I'm preparing myself to go back to the front lines, wherever that unknown location may be.

Without your letters, I'm at a loss to know what your plans are for the summer. My guess is you'll loaf for a few weeks before you begin working. At least you should loaf until loafing becomes work. I know your letters are hung up somewhere, and I know that reading them would be the best treatment I could get. I'm feeling much better and am able to walk around a bit now. I want to be with you so very much, Ginny. I know, though, that it will all be worth waiting for. And nothing will disturb my patience or my ability to wait.

༶

June 25, 1945

𝒟ear Ginny,

It's getting lonely here. Can't talk with the guys I fought alongside, and can't talk with you. I put in a request to track down my mail. Hope somebody finds it. Your words might be the cure I'm waiting for.

༶

July 3, 1945

𝒟ear Ginny,

I thought and thought about how I could adequately express the happiness you gave me today—for your letter of May 21st arrived. It's the first in over a month. I love you so very dearly. I've got to tell you that right off the bat. Thank you so very much. Your letter is like 24-karat gold.

I met one of the fellows who was hurt after I was, and his report on casualties wasn't good. Very few men in our company are left, and none from my platoon. It hurts. We were about to push the enemy into the sea at the end of the island when I left, and we had already felt the brunt of their frantic suicidal attacks. No doubt this type of attack was responsible for the casualties. No doubt, also, Okinawa was expensive. There are many Japanese that are no more. I'll never forget the faces of the soldiers who died while fighting with me. I feel so sorry for their families. And Okinawa, the most important base in the Pacific, is ours.

I like the infantry and the men. I guess seventy days of fighting was enough for me to say I'm fortunately alive and in one piece. So I must be thankful to God.

Hope the horse show was a success and that you came out on top (as usual). Glad mother and dad were able to go. Mother wrote (a letter I received at the same time as yours) that they were eager to go and watch you perform.

Yesterday, I put my clothes on for the first time and managed to get around quite a bit. I attended a movie and did some reading at the Red Cross center. The walking itself was refreshing. The doctor said I am definitely showing improvement.

How thankful I am—mostly to you, my darling, knowing your prayers meant so very much. Our faith will always keep us happy. I'll write again soon. And remember, you have my deepest love.

༄

July 3, 1945

Dear Mother & Dad,
Today was a gala day, for I received a letter from you and one from Ginny, the first letters in over a month.

You sound very happy, and that makes me happy, especially to know you're not worrying about me. Also, good to know the farm is showing its practical usefulness now....

The doctors say I'll be here for a while longer, then sent to Hawaii and assigned to non-combat duty. How does that sound!....

Ginny's letter was a great comfort to me. I really missed her letters, as I did yours. The time together with Ginny was all too short, and I'm real anxious to be with her again...

Thanks for Dick's address. Even in his overseas duty, he will always be comfortable on a ship – with hot food and a bunk. Yes, the Lang family should be thankful all the way around....

Will close for now....Love.

ᔂ

July 8, 1945

Dear Ginny,

I went to another movie a couple of nights ago, and a crazy thing happened. It seems that I lapsed back into real restless nights where I keep trying to fight off depression that I thought I'd gotten away from. Talking to the doctor that had hypnotized me about this, he wanted to know about the movie. It was a western movie. We discovered that the terrain was similar to Okinawa and in a gunfight some men were trapped in a ravine, in a small stream, desperately trying to get out. He tried to draw out of me an experience that might relate. Well, through some manipulations, he finally got me to remember an experience I had sheltered in my mind. It was an experience that I had chosen to forget, because I felt so helpless. I was just utterly helpless.

Well, he told me to face up to it, it was part of my life, and he said that very sympathetically, for he is a very caring guy. Why don't you write a letter about it, he said. Share the experience. So, here it is, Ginny.

Our platoon had just finished a successful operation by securing a real strategic position on top of one of the highest points on the island. Beyond this point there was a stretch of flat land leading to the next hill. The only approach was to spread out abreast and run. In the middle, all of a sudden, we all fell into a ditch about six-feet deep with about two feet of water. The Japs had camouflaged the ditch with tree branches, or whatever, and we just fell into their trap.

Hidden at the end of the ditch, a Jap machine gun began firing down the center. Some of us could protect ourselves by hugging the bank. But not all of us. Then the mortar shells started to fall. By submerging ourselves in the water, with our weapons held over our heads, some of us could avoid the shrapnel. Again, but not all of us. So, alternately, we were hugging the bank and falling in the water. I kept trying to make contact with the company command post with my radio, but I couldn't get reception down in this ditch. When I put the radio up above the ditch, I drew small arms fire from the hill beyond. Finally, I made contact and asked for tank fire at the end of the ditch to stop the machine gun and on the hill to stop the mortars and small arms fire. They said it would take time to bring the tanks. Then I asked for some smoke so it would drift across our position. With that, we could climb out and run back. I passed the word along the ditch to be ready for the smoke and before climbing out to make sure that each man who looked dead really was dead and that the wounded be carried out. After some problems in adjusting the smoke, it finally drifted by, and we moved out to our original starting point. I ran with my arm around my wounded man, with his shattered elbow hanging by a thread.

We dug foxholes facing out to that ditch. The Jap fire had stopped. Shortly, night began to fall. All seemed quiet. Then from the ditch came cries, saying, "Help Me, Help Me" every few minutes. And we sat there helpless. The cries lasted most of the night, each series of cries becoming further and further apart. Near morning they stopped. Did we leave some wounded, or was this a Jap trick?

At dawn, orders came down to flank that ditch area. We were going around it. In fact, the entire battalion went around it. Walking away was hard to take. So was that memory.

You have become part of my recovery process, Ginny. Now, instead of suppressing that memory, it's become important always to remember it in respect to those men of mine in that ditch. We will do that together.

I'm going to rest now, turning my thoughts around from the past to the future. That future we've been dreaming about. Love you.

ح

July 15, 1945

*D*ear Ginny,

I'm awfully sorry, Ginny, for failing to write these past few days. It isn't that I haven't been thinking of you, for you're in my most cherished thoughts each moment of the day. I've received thirteen letters from you, and you'll never under-stand (until I return) how much each word of them has meant to me. A bunch of them were written in May when you were in school, plus your most recent ones from June and July. I put them all together in order, then I read them all at once to see if there was some kind of overall effect. You're probably thinking I have nothing better to do with my time.

I'm awfully proud of the results of the horse show. Mother and dad were pleased also. They said you appeared very pretty in your riding outfit, darling, and I've tried to picture to myself how you must have looked.

Right now, I'm standing by for a plane or a ship to Hawaii. I will be there in a Naval hospital under recommen-dation of reassigning to duty other than line combat. The doctor said that another blast concussion may prove much more serious next time. I'm sorry. You know how much I love the infantry and that type of life. During combat there was a thrill in the spirit of fighting and a feeling of satisfaction that results from a tough job. I was fighting for something that was worthwhile. And the spirit of the Marines in battle is something like playing football for your alma mater. You learn a lot about teamwork. I've seen and experienced a lot—perhaps enough. This looks like the end of my infantry days.

I met a very good friend from Colgate here. He's here, too, as a result of Okinawa. And we have been spending time together. In the evenings we attend the movies (you bring your own bucket to sit on). Then we return to his ward for coffee. We take our cups outside on the steps overlooking the wilderness of Saipan and watch the searchlights rake the terrain, looking for Japanese. Part of the area here is still infested with a few enemy soldiers hiding out in caves. They're the ones who stayed behind when their buddies were chased off this island by our Marines. They cause very little trouble, but they are still ready to attack anyone who walks around unprotected.

On the steps we talk over old times at school, hash over our combat experiences, and always end up talking about Jenny (his) and Ginny (mine). I'm feeling well lately. I only have spells occasionally now, which means improvement. Be sure to send me your graduation picture when I arrive in Hawaii. But wait until I send an address that I'm sure of. Speaking of graduation, darling, I've made you a little something in the craft shop that I'll send you tomorrow. I've rambled on quite a bit it seems, so I'll close for now. I love you so. I thank God each night for finding someone so kind, considerate, so beautifully sincere and pure, so pleasant to dream about.

ॐ

Author's Note: It occurred to me, are we ever going to be friendly to the Japanese again? How can we? Look what they've done to me, all those men, my friends, the anguish of their loved ones.

July 18, 1945

Dear Ginny,

War news is encouraging. I'll be so very glad when I don't have to see a Japanese face again. It seems that every movie I watch here has something in it about the war and the Japanese. Even the Japanese girls who work around here bother me, and I find it very hard to be friendly to them. Of course, I realize they are too young and ill-informed to be guilty of anything. But enough of that!

I'm still standing by for a plane or a ship to Hawaii. I'd like to start work on something, for time hangs heavy around here. Maybe a woodworking project would keep me calm and focused. Lights are about to go out, my darling. I'll be holding you so very close to me, looking into your eyes saying how very much I love you.

∾

July 23, 1945

Dear Mother & Dad,

I've been reluctant about my correspondence lately, mainly I guess, because there is so very little to write about. I'm still waiting transportation to Hawaii. I didn't figure on waiting this long. I believe a flu epidemic in Hawaii is holding things up. Also, it's been quite some time since I've had any mail, and I feel lost without it.

Greg Batt, my friend from Colgate, with whom I've spent a lot of time together, left this morning back to duty, going to Guam.

The war news is encouraging. I firmly believe the end is in sight, and next summer we will all be together at the farm....Love.

∾

July 24, 1945

Dear Ginny,

I'm leaving in a few minutes for Hawaii by plane. Each day brings us nearer to each other. I'll send along my new address as soon as I know it.

Part 8

Naval Hospital In Honolulu
July 1945 — August 1945

July 26, 1945

$\mathcal{D}$ear Ginny,

If you've ever seen the proverbial hillbilly looking open-mouthed at the tall buildings and confusion of New York City not knowing what to make of it all, you can understand my feelings today. Though Hawaii is no New York City, this weapon-less existence is such a far cry from where I've been that it's difficult to believe that I'm actually here with all of the comforts and pleasures at my disposal. No noise of gun-fire. No looking over my shoulder.

On Okinawa you feel that life such as this no longer existed—that life is only a fight from hill to hill with a meal of rations in between.

I finally shed my dungarees, having been issued some khaki. With this address now, darling, you can send me your graduation picture with comparative assurance that it will arrive. And please don't forget those snapshots, too. I'll always await your letters. During the days of combat, faith in your love and faith in the goodness of God kept me going with an energy I'd have found no other place. It still and always will hold true. I'll close for now, darling. Think I'll take a little walk and then go to bed. Good-night, Ginny.

ᵌᵔ

July 26, 1945

$\mathcal{D}$ear Mother & Dad,
Like Cinderella, I feel unbelievably transformed here in

Hawaii. In 24 hours, as if by magic, the crudeness, the wilderness, and the forever lingering Japanese flavor have all disappeared. And in their place, peace and civilized life. Like stop lights, sidewalks, civilian cars, homes, buses, street lights, women, milk, beer, liquor, milk shakes – a weapon-less existence. To tell the truth, I'm so amazed, I can't believe it. As a matter of fact, I haven't taken advantage of much yet. Today, I've been merely admiring. Like looking at a decorated cake, almost too beautiful to eat. While on the battlefields of Okinawa, you feel that things such as these fail to exist, or at least you've forgotten, and that the world is only a fight for hill after hill with a meal of cold rations in between. That's not inconceivable when you consider you've had to be alert every minute for almost two and a half months, being in a dirt hole every night, carrying your rifle like it was part of your body, wearing the same clothes, unbathed, wondering if you'll ever have a hot meal.

I arrived here early this morning by plane, virtually without a personal possession. Sort of starting from scratch. Ran into a couple of fellows I knew on Okinawa already. Better get some things done and will write again soon....Love.

გ

July 30, 1945

Dear Ginny,

The word is that the wounded here will be coming home. In the service, Ginny, you know how uncertain expectations may be. And in my case, I won't be certain until the orders are issued.

Maybe you could put off getting a steady job at the present time. Because, upon arrival in the States, I may possibly receive leave. That way, we'd have our days together, darling, and we'd be able to do over and over again all those things we've been dreaming of all these long months. But as I say, Ginny, we must wait and be sure before our hopes are raised too high. I ought to know in about a week. We'll keep our fingers crossed.

Today is a rainy afternoon. I'd like, of course, to be able to hear those raindrops on the roof of the farmhouse with us inside dressed in lazy clothes just fooling around playing records—with nothing for us to do but be together. Maybe, maybe not so long from now.

ॐ

August 5, 1945

Dear Mother & Dad,
I might as well start right out and tell you that it looks as though I'll be coming home. About a week ago, I was told of this, but it sounded too good to be true. I didn't want to say anything — although I did mention to Ginny that it might happen. That's because I hoped Ginny wouldn't get a steady job, there being the possibility I would be getting leave. Truthfully, I never expected to be sent home. I thought I'd be reassigned somewhere else in the world. I was just con-

tent with the thought of merely being alive and on my own two feet....

Coming back to my quarters yesterday, I found an enve-lope from you on my bed – your Easter card. It was dated March 26th. Easter was April 1st, the day we landed on Okinawa. We'll always remember that Easter.... Will close for now with the happy thought of seeing you soon....Love.

๛

August 8, 1945

𝒟ear Ginny,

Still no word on going home. The wait for orders continues.

By coincidence, I met one of my best and oldest friends from home here at the officers club. We've been spending some time together swimming and drinking beer. I obtained leave from the hospital, and we're going to an officers rest camp for a few days—just to lie around on the beach as well as play a little tennis. We used to work in the same summer camp.

Also, I met a fellow from my platoon who was shot in the rear end. He is pretty well healed up now, and yesterday we went to Waikiki for lunch and a swim. He was one of my best machine gunners and one of the two I put up for the sil-ver star. Hope he gets it. I'm sure he will.

Darling, I can hardly wait to see you. Before, I felt deter-mined to wait for peace, but now with it close, I'm sitting on pins and needles. It's going to be wonderful. I'll close for now, Ginny. I'll hop in bed and fall off to sleep dreaming of us close together and content with our love.

꙳

August 14, 1945

𝒟ear Ginny,

The good news is that I feel much better. Headaches are few and far between. Plus, I've learned to ignore the nightmares. The bad news is that there is still no word on when I leave for the states. I feel a bit of jealousy, because my buddy shipped out for California yesterday. But I'll be patient. We have a lifetime to look forward to.

꙳

August 20, 1945

𝒟ear Mother & Dad,

Received a letter from you today. It took me out of a blue mood. The delay of waiting for my orders gets to me, being lonelier than ever for home.

Glad to know you are both well. So the vegetable garden is going to be ripe for me? Dad, that sounds great. And, mother, you know how much I'm looking forward to your cooking.

As to your question, the pain in my head and abdomen are only occasional now and not very severe. I weigh 160 and still retain my mustache....

When I think about it, I've been fortunate to have this opportunity to indoctrinate myself here before coming home. Particularly, taming down my Marine Corps vocabulary. Foxhole words are best left in foxholes....Love.

ॐ

Author's Note: The joyous thought of going home, of seeing Ginny, of seeing my mother and dad is mingled with the thought of leaving behind the men of the third platoon and my fellow officers, living and dying together. How can I forget them? Never. Our experiences will live as part of me the rest of my life. And what happened to Bill Terry, Norm White, Jake, Doc, and Scotty? Such great friends. Will we ever see each other again? Fortunately, my brother, Dick, is O.K.

August 21, 1945

Dear Ginny,

Well, the orders finally came. I'm going home. Two other fellows and I are boarding a liner on the 25th. Also, this afternoon I was called to the commanding officer's office, where he decorated me with the Purple Heart medal. I'm very proud of it, Ginny. When I'm home, we'll get all dressed up some night, and I'll wear it. On top of that, I ran into my brother, Dick. We've been spending some time together until last night. His ship left this morning. Sure was good to see him, Ginny. It was a stroke of luck. I have just finished writing a letter to mother and dad telling them about it.

Darling, seven of your letters arrived, and also your picture. And it's a beautiful picture, Ginny. It appears so real. I like your hair short like that. Darling, I can hardly wait to be with you again. Sorry to keep you waiting like this, but it can't be long now. I bought a nice leather frame for the picture. I feel so very close to you, as if we've known each other all of our lives. And I've written a little poem to express the way I feel.

I love you, Ginny, because God made it so
He made it for me to hold you close
Never to let you go.

I love you, Ginny, because of what you are
Mostly when you're near
More than ever when you're afar.

With that thought, I'll sign off for tonight, darling. Looks like it'll be the end of summer by the time I can kiss you. We'll be able to initiate the arrival of autumn. It will be a beautiful season for us. Saddle up. We'll be riding in the fields again.

ॐ

Upon his return to the United States, Second Lieutenant Harry O. Lang, Jr. was awarded the Bronze Star for bravery by President Harry S. Truman. The citation reads:

"For heroic achievement as a Platoon Leader of Company E, Second Battalion, Seventh Marines, First Marine Division, in action against enemy Japanese forces on Okinawa, Ryukyu Islands, 12 May 1945. When the rifle company to which he was attached was halted by heavy enemy artillery fire during the attack on Dakeshi Ridge, Second Lieutenant Lang moved up under intense hostile machine-gun and mortar fire with the men of his platoon and, skillfully directing their deployment and fire, led them into the assault on a key hill which, when taken, secured the flank of the company and covered its advance. By his initiative and courageous leadership, Second Lieutenant Lang contributed materially to the rapid advance of the company with minimum losses, and his devotion to duty was in keeping with the highest traditions of the United States Naval Service. Second Lieutenant Lang is authorized to wear the Combat "V"."

Epilogue

$\mathcal{H}$arry and Ginny did ride together again, galloping across fields blazing with red and yellow. A year after he returned home, in September of 1946, they were married and soon after built their own special dream house in Farmington Hills, Michigan—the white house with green shutters that Harry had conjured up in his poem.

They had a son and a daughter and were living the life they had boldly hoped for when, one day after planting roses, Harry went to the mailbox and found orders calling him back to active duty for the Korean War. Ironically, his orders again placed him at Camp Pendleton (and in the same tent camp) training rifle platoons and writing letters to Ginny by candlelight. Harry found he had been wrong about one thing in his previous wartime letters. Those pre-war thirty days with Ginny, which he had referred to as his favorite memories, had proved to be only the beginning. Now his memories encompassed Ginny, their two young children, and the dream they had made a reality.

Fortunate again, Harry completed his Marine Corps duties stateside and returned home to Ginny and his young family. The next few years brought three more daughters. The family spent their summers sailing and golfing, autumns horseback riding, and winters skiing—all the things Harry had imagined back in those foxholes on Okinawa.

Looking back over Harry's letters, Ginny recalls how the recognition of mortality was heightened in all Americans during the war, perhaps making people more honest with their beliefs, their emotions, and the words they used when communicating to members of our fighting forces. The American soldier, as well, Ginny recalls, rarely talked in circles.

She can remember feeling "overcome" when she received the letter where Harry, for the first time, declared his love for her. "Until that point, I wasn't completely sure how Harry felt," she admits. "Our relationship really developed through the letters." And, she adds, "A lot towards the end was built on memory—and faith."

That faith in each other has sustained them through life's ups and downs and through close to fifty-two years of marriage. Now, fifty-four years after the first letter, Harry and Ginny have moved north to Traverse City, on the shores of Lake Michigan, where they are visited regularly by their five children and twelve grandchildren.

As for Jake, Doc, Scotty, Norman White, Bill Terry and Harry's brother: amazingly, they all made it through the war. Harry remains close with Norman White, his friend since high school. And a few years ago, when Bill Terry, his training camp roommate, passed away, Harry delivered the eulogy at his funeral. He talked of their early days together as two young Marines fighting brutal battles for their country, yet forging lifelong friendships.

Epilogue

Harry's mother and dad shared 55 years, spending happy and contented years on the farm, always looking forward to the many joyous family visits.

Although Harry and Ginny describe themselves as "just a couple of normal people" who happened to go through the same experience that thousands of others went through during World War II, both agree that sharing the experience of love and war is unique, particularly when the love becomes everlasting—and stays ever new.